*"Skate to w...
is goi...
not where it has been."*

—Wayne Gretzky, reciting his father's advice

HOCKEY
QUOTES

compiled by

J. Alexander Poulton

OVER
TIME
BOOKS

The Publisher: OverTime Books is an imprint of Éditions de la Montagne Verte
Website: www.overtimebooks.com

Library and Archives Canada Cataloguing in Publication

Poulton, J. Alexander (Jay Alexander), 1977–
    Hockey quotes / J. Alexander Poulton.

ISBN 13: 978-1-897277-35-5
ISBN 10: 1-897277-35-0

      1. Hockey players—Quotations. 2. Hockey coaches—Quotations.
3. Hockey—Quotations, maxims, etc. I. Title.

GV847.P69 2008   796.96202   C2008-903523-2

Project Director: J. Alexander Poulton
Editor: Timothy Niedermann
Production: Jodene Draven
Cover Image: Courtesy of Photos.com

We acknowledge the financial support of the Government of Canada through the Book Publishing Industry Development Program for our publishing activities.

Canadian   Patrimoine
Heritage   canadien

PC: 6

CONTENTS

DEDICATION

To all the reporters who furiously scribble down just about everything the players, coaches and everyone involved in the game says.

INTRODUCTION

If anyone represents the qualities we associate with hockey, it is Pittsburgh Penguins great Mario Lemieux. Whether facing season-ending injuries or battling cancer, Mario Lemieux has always returned to the game he loves and has proved that he is a true gentleman of hockey, who played more for the passion of pure sport than for the money that came with it.

In the following book, you will find all sorts of quotations about the game of hockey. From the first stars of the game to those of the present, from average fans to Hollywood stars, you will discover the many different ways that the game of hockey has touched people's lives.

Reading these quotations, you will get a greater sense of how hockey has become something more than a simple sport to the people who have invested their lives in its pursuit. Through the words of Wayne Gretzky, Sidney Crosby, Maurice Richard and others, you will see the game from the point of view of those who have dedicated themselves to it and whose lives are played out on the rink for all the world to see.

Going through some of the more famous quotations, such as Foster Hewitt's description of Paul Henderson's 1972 Summit Series game-winning goal or Al Michaels's call of "Do you believe in miracles?" when the United States rallied to beat the Soviets in the 1980 Olympics, you begin to realize that these words have not only marked the history of the game but also the story of our lives. These words unite every hockey fan through the shared experience of those moments of hockey greatness. It is why we watch the game and why we return each season for more because, as Mario Lemieux says, "Every day is a great day for hockey."

THE MOST FAMOUS

Through these famous phrases we see the history of the game. How many remember where they were when they heard Foster Hewitt call Paul Henderson's goal in the 1972 Summit Series or who can forget the words of wisdom from Wayne Gretzky on how to play the game? Words that have now become legend.

I have for some time been thinking that it would be a good thing if there were a challenge cup, which would be held from year to year by the leading hockey club in the Dominion. Considering the general interest which hockey matches now elicit, and the importance of having the game played fairly and under rules generally recognized, I am willing to give a cup which shall be held from year to year by the winning club.

–Lord Frederick Arthur Stanley (1841–1908), governor general of Canada, in a letter to a friend

Skate to where the puck is going to be, not where it has been.

–Wayne Gretzky (1961–), NHL great, reciting his father's advice

If you can't beat 'em in the alley, you'll never beat them on the ice.

–Conn Smythe (1895–1980), Toronto Maple Leafs owner and hockey builder

He Shoots! He Scores!

–Foster Hewitt (1902–85), Canadian hockey broadcaster

Cannonading Drives!
Booming Blasts!
Scintillating Saves!
Negotiating contact with the puck!
Savardian Spinnerama!

–Danny Gallivan (1917–93), Canadian sportscaster, just a sample
of his many neologisms

For the benefit of Wayne Gretzky, my new wife and our
expected child in the new year, it would be beneficial for
everyone involved to let me play with the Los Angeles Kings.

–Wayne Gretzky (1961–), NHL great, announcing that he was
being traded to Los Angeles, August 9, 1988

To the people across Canada, we're trying our best. For the
people who booed us, geez, I'm really…all of the guys are
really disheartened and we're disillusioned and disappointed
in some of the people. We cannot believe the bad press we've
got…the booing in our own buildings. Every one of us guys,
35 guys, who came out to play for Team Canada, we did it
because we love our country and not for any other reason.
And even though we play in the United States and we earn
money in the United States, Canada is still our home, and
that's the only reason we come. And I don't think it's fair that
we should be booed.

–Phil Esposito (1942–), Boston Bruins great, during the
1972 Summit Series against the Soviet Union

No one wants us to win except the guys on this team and our
fans, but we're a proud team and we're still standing. It turns
my stomach to hear some of the things being said about us.
To a man, every one of our guys will say how great Hašek or
Sundin is. I don't think we dislike the other countries nearly
as much as they hate us.

–Wayne Gretzky (1961–), NHL great, on Team Canada at the
2002 Winter Olympics

For every $250 I fined him, Québec businessmen would send him $1000. Richard could do no wrong in Québec. I was always the villain.

–Clarence Campbell (1905–84), NHL president,
on Maurice Richard

Wow, that kid just took off like a rocket!

–Ray Getliffe (1914–2008), Montréal Canadiens left winger, as he watched the young Maurice Richard in practice. Montréal *Gazette* reporter Dink Carroll overheard this and used it the next day in his column. "Rocket" became Richard's nickname after that.

This record honors all French Canadians.

–Maurice Richard (1921–2000), Montréal Canadiens great, on scoring his 45th goal of the 1944–45 season and breaking the previous season-goal-scoring record set by Joe Malone

Do you believe in miracles?

–Al Michaels (1944–), American sportscaster, after the U.S. hockey team defeated the Soviets in the 1980 Olympic semifinals

Sixty minutes of Hell!

–Glenn Hall (1931–), Chicago Blackhawks goaltender,
on playing goal

In the future, they can fall on their knees, or stand on their heads, if they think they can stop the puck better in that way than by standing on their feet.

–Frank Calder (1877–1943), first NHL president, on changing the rules to allow goaltenders to fall to the ice to make a save. Prior to this, goaltenders were given a two-minute penalty for making a save on their knees.

THE GAME

Hockey can mean something different to each person, yet we are all united by the game. It can stir such feelings of passion and fond memories in us all. These are just a few words from hockey's most famous adherents.

Baseball can have its perfect dimensions, its undeniable drama, but hockey, for all its wrongs, still has the potential to deliver a momentary, flashing magic that is found in no other game we play.

–Roy MacGregor (1948–), Canadian writer
and newspaper columnist

Basketball, hockey and track meets are action heaped upon action, climax upon climax, until the onlooker's responses become deadened. Baseball is for the leisurely afternoons of summer and for the unchanging dreams.

–Roger Kahn (1927–), American sportswriter

Baseball happens to be a game of cumulative tension, but football, basketball and hockey are played with hand grenades and machine guns.

–John Leonard (1939–), American writer and critic

But I smile at the small-town myth for the harmless, happy days it gave me, and God knows how many tens of thousands of others. Hockey, for most of us, was the first time—and so often the only time—we ever felt we truly mattered.

–Ken Dryden (1947–), Montréal Canadiens Hall of Fame goaltender

The equipment that stayed up on the shelf has come down again. The boy becomes a man; the player, a fan; a coach, a father, now a player again; and the game goes on.

–Roy MacGregor (1948–), Canadian writer and newspaper columnist

It was for self-preservation. I got sick of taking him to the park and sitting there for hours freezing to death.

–Walter Gretzky (1938–), father of Wayne, about building an outdoor hockey rink for his son

Car!

–Any kid playing street hockey

Throughout the years ahead, just as in the past, NHL hockey will remain one of the most exciting team games, an awesome exhibition of strength, speed, endurance and fitness wherever it is played.

–Brian McFarlane (1931–), Canadian sportswriter and broadcaster

There is only one way a boy can be sure to learn to play hockey—on the pond, on the creek, on a flooded lot. The foundation of hockey isn't really hockey at all. It's shinny, a wild melee of kids batting a puck around, with no rules, no organization—nothing but individual effort to grab and old the puck.

–Lester Patrick (1883–1960), NHL player, coach, general manager and hockey builder

You can't play hockey if you're nice.

–Steve Ludzik (1961–), Tampa Bay Lightning head coach

In the old days, you could have a guy who couldn't do anything but fight because he wouldn't hurt you too much on the ice. But with the up-and-down of the game now, you have to be able to do more than fight. Plus, with the salary cap, you can't afford to keep around guys who fight and don't do much else. You watch. In a couple of seasons, there will hardly be any fights at all. That's where the game is headed.

–Phil Esposito (1942–), Boston Bruins great

Sources also confirm that there is no one left in Canada who can remember when hockey was a simple game, played for fun.

–Roy MacGregor (1948–), Canadian writer and newspaper columnist, on contract talks with Alexei Yashin

Hockey is the only job I know where you get paid to have a nap on the day of the game.

–Chico Resch (1948–), New York Islanders goaltender

My father used to tell me the game is not privileged to have you, you're privileged to have hockey.

–Paul Coffey (1961–), Edmonton Oilers defenseman

You have to know what pro hockey is all about. You have to live and breathe and sleep it. You have to lose a few teeth and take some shots to the face. It's not a pretty thing.

–Ted Nolan (1958–), New York Islanders head coach

We know that hockey is where we live, where we can best meet and overcome pain and wrong and death. Life is just a place where we spend time between games.

–Fred Shero (1925–90), Philadelphia Flyers head coach

Sporting games will probably always continue to rise and fall in popularity, but a select few are destined to become a medium through which human beings define themselves and indeed exceed themselves. Ice hockey, a passionate, high-octane sport with millions of faithful fans around the globe, belongs to that elite club. From its humble beginnings as a game played with sticks and stones on the frozen bogs of pioneer Canada, it has metamorphosed into a sophisticated test of mental and physical agility. It is difficult to find a sport that has lasted for more than 110 years. And its traditions live on. The annual matches between the first two teams in Kingston, Ontario—the hockey players of the Royal Military College and Queen's University—continue to this day.

—Introduction to *Kings of the Ice: A History of World Hockey*

People didn't know the difference between a blue line and a clothes line.

—Al Michaels (1944–), American sportscaster, describing Americans' knowledge of hockey prior to the 1980 Miracle on Ice

Hockey belongs to the Cartoon Network, where a person can be pancaked by an Acme anvil, then expanded, accordion-style, back to full stature, without any lasting side effect.

—Steve Rushin (1966–), American sportswriter

There's more violence in one football game than there is in an entire hockey season, and nobody ever talks about that.

—Keith Allen (1923–), Detroit Red Wings defenseman

You can have all the talent in the world, but if the pumper's not there, it doesn't matter.

—Glen Sather (1943–), Edmonton Oilers head coach

I prefer the NHL style of hockey. You always think European hockey is going to be more wide open and with more scoring and that sort of stuff, but it's almost the opposite. There is less scoring.…There was a lot more grabbing, holding and clutching than I expected. Because of the big ice, there's a lot of man-on-man play. In the playoffs, they were just draped all over me, and nothing got called. They let everything go. I remember forwards looking at me and not even looking at the play, with their stick between my legs.

–Dan Boyle (1976–), Tampa Bay Lightning defenseman, on his season spent in Sweden during the 2004–05 lockout

I didn't really want to play, but in the back of your mind you always want to play, if that makes any sense. I don't think anybody retires without still wanting to play. I'll always want to play.

–Mark Messier (1961–), NHL great, on his retirement

The winters of my childhood were long, long seasons. We lived in three places—the school, the church and the skating rink—but our real life was on the skating rink.

–Roch Carrier (1937–), Canadian writer

I don't think any one person will ever be bigger than the game.

–Wayne Gretzky (1961–), NHL great

I get goosebumps when we come out and hear the fans cheering and the music playing loud.

–Rick Nash (1984–), Columbus Blue Jackets left winger

Perhaps Mario Lemieux and Paul Coffey as well. Those guys were probably my favorite players growing up. I enjoy playing defense. I don't see myself ever changing positions.

–Scott Niedermayer (1973–), Anaheim Ducks defenseman,
looking back on his early days

I wasn't crazy about it at first, but I was one of the strongest kids at skating backwards.

–Eric Brewer (1979–), St. Louis Blues defenseman,
on why he plays defense

It got so bad that I couldn't sleep on the night before a game. I couldn't even keep my meals down.

–Bill Durnan (1916–72), Montréal Canadiens goaltending legend,
on the pressures of the game

I don't get too concerned about the game. I go out there and really enjoy myself. I don't make it hard on myself. I don't put extra pressure on myself. When you are full of confidence, I think it helps you play a lot of games. You don't feel the pressure. That's when a goalie gets tired—when they feel the pressure.

–Martin Brodeur (1972–), New Jersey Devils goaltender

I've always felt hockey was like a disease. You can't really shake it.

–Ken Wregget (1964–), Pittsburgh Penguins goaltender

Hockey is a man's game. The team with the most real men wins.

–Brian Burke (1955–), Anaheim Ducks general manager,

Hockey is like a religion in Montréal. You're either a saint or a sinner; there's no in-between.

–Patrick Roy (1965–), Montréal Canadiens goaltender

THE GREATEST

For every generation there is a player that stands out among the crowd and achieves the status of a legend. Be it Howie Morenz, Maurice Richard, Gordie Howe, Terry Sawchuk, Jean Beliveau, Guy Lafleur, Wayne Gretzky, Mario Lemieux or Sidney Crosby, all these players are united by their passion for the game.

I may not be the hockey player Jean Beliveau was, but some day I hope to be the man he is.

—Guy Lafleur (1951–), Montréal Canadiens right winger

If I can be half the hockey player that Bobby Orr was, I'll be happy.

—Ray Bourque (1960–), Boston Bruins defenseman

I don't think you ever stopped Bobby Orr; you contained Bobby Orr, but you NEVER stopped him!

—Larry Robinson (1951–), Montréal Canadiens defenseman

No question about it, he's the finest player I've ever seen.

—Lynn Patrick (1912–80), Boston Bruins general manager,
on Jean Beliveau

There ought to be two leagues, one for the pros and one for Beliveau.

—Dollard St. Laurent (1929–), Montréal Canadiens defenseman,
on teammate Jean Beliveau

I remember the day of his last radiation treatment. He went to Philly. He got there about four o'clock, and he played. I think he gets overlooked, what he's overcome. It's ridiculous. Everybody talks about Michael Jordan coming back from baseball, but Mario came back from cancer.

–Kevin Stevens (1965–), Pittsburgh Penguins left winger, on teammate Mario Lemieux coming back after beating cancer.

It had been a great career. I mean, how many guys can say they averaged two points a game in their careers? It's too bad he's retiring too soon. The league is going to miss him. The fans are going to miss him. A real classy person and a great guy.

–Johnny Bucyk (1935–), Boston Bruins right winger, on Mario Lemieux's first retirement

The finest athlete of them all, that's what Gordie is. And when I say athlete I'm talking about any sport. Take everything into consideration: his age, his record, his condition. There are some pretty good athletes around, great boxers, great football players, everything, but Gordie is in a league by himself. I'd be proud to be half the man on or off the ice that Gordie is.

–Bobby Orr (1948–), Boston Bruins defenseman, on hockey legend Gordie Howe

I retired in 1971, the same year Guy arrived, and he came to me and asked me what I thought about him taking **my** sweater number. "If you want it, take it," I told him, "but don't you think you already have enough on you? Why don't you pick another number and make it famous yourself?"

–Jean Beliveau (1931–), Montréal Canadiens center, on Guy Lafleur

The greatest hockey player who ever lived: Bobby Orr, and I love him.

–Don Cherry (1934–), Canadian hockey commentator

I can relate to Mario, because I played with him. But Bobby Hull? Guys like him are kind of gods. Their 600 goals are different from the 600 goals I have. They played fewer games, and it was more defensive then.

—Steve Yzerman (1965–), Detroit Red Wings center, on entering into the top 10 scorers of all-time

He could shoot harder than anybody I see nowadays. When he'd wind up behind that net he wasn't number 7, he was number 777, just a blur.

—Roy "Shrimp" Worters (1900–57), NHL Hall of Fame goaltender, on Howie Morenz

I played with him but not exactly with him, if you get what I mean. I was always in front of him or behind him. I could never stay even with him, that's for sure. Jesus Christ, could he go! End-to-end rushes….None of this back-and-forth passing to get there, he went straight from end-to-end.

—Aurel Joliat (1901–86), Montréal Canadiens left winger, on teammate Howie Morenz

Morenz was the greatest I ever saw. He was as fast as a bullet and had a shot to match. He could stop on a dime and give you five cents change. The first time I played against him he sifted right through the Ottawa defense and scored. I said to him, "Kid, you do that again, and I'll cut your legs off." He said to me, "Clancy, I'll be right back." Seconds later, there he was again, cutting right between my partner and me and scoring again. I couldn't believe the little bugger could move that fast.

—Francis Michael "King" Clancy (1903–86), NHL player, coach and executive, on Howie Morenz

When Richard scored his 50 goals, he gave us all hope. French Canadians are no longer to be condemned to be hewers of wood and drawers of water, to be servants, employees. We, too, are champions of the world.

—Roch Carrier (1937–), Canadian writer, on Maurice Richard when he scored 50 goals in 50 games in the 1944–45 season

Rocket had that mean look in every game we played. He was 100 percent hockey. He could hate with the best of them.

—Gordie Howe (1928–), Detroit Red Wings great, on Maurice Richard

I tried to size him up, but I couldn't. He'd score on me through my legs, then another along the ice, then on one side, and then on the other side. He had me going crazy. The biggest thrill of my life was when he retired.

—Johnny Bower (1924–), Toronto Maple Leafs goaltender, on Maurice Richard

From the blue line in, I never saw a player as exciting as Richard. When he had the goalie beat, he finished it off, and you had no chance to recover.

—Emile Francis (1936–), Toronto Maple Leafs goaltender, on Maurice Richard

To play so well and for so long is simply incredible. No player will ever do the things in hockey that Gordie did.

—Wayne Gretzky (1961–), NHL great, on his hero Gordie Howe

Since the beginning, I always loved the game. When you grow up in Montréal, one day you want to be a professional hockey player. When I was six or seven, I knew that was what I wanted.

—Mario Lemieux (1965–), Pittsburgh Penguins great

I'm not sure Mario is going to get the accolades he deserves, especially from outside the game. But from within, the players, the people who follow closely, realize exactly what he's brought to the table, exactly what he has done. People tend to forget…hockey was dying in Pittsburgh before he got there. I played there. It was almost dead. I'm sorry, but the NHL would not have a franchise in Pittsburgh today had Mario not come along. Think about it, no hockey in Pittsburgh.

–Wayne Gretzky (1961–), NHL great, on Mario Lemieux

On sheer ability, Mario is good enough to win scoring titles with a broken stick. On pure talent, he's the best there is. But Wayne almost never disappoints you. He comes to work every night.

–Bobby Orr (1948–), Boston Bruins defenseman

When he broke in with us, he was basically a one-dimensional player. He could shoot the puck, and he could do it better than anybody. But he wasn't great defensively, he had trouble turning, he wasn't strong and his skating had to be improved. He just got better every season, to the point where he became one of the greatest defensemen to ever play the game.

–Cliff Fletcher (1935–), Calgary Flames general manager,
on Al MacInnis

He had the talent for everything. How big he is, how he protects the puck, his hands, how smart he is on the ice, all the plays he made. He was always the smartest player on the ice. For him, it's pretty natural. If I'm off a week, I have trouble skating my first three days back. With him, it's easy. It's just natural ability.

–Vincent Lecavalier (1980–), Tampa Bay Lightning forward,
on Mario Lemieux

My two most important games in my career were my first
game against Mario [Lemieux] and my first game against
Wayne Gretzky.

–Daniel Brière (1977–), Philadelphia Flyers center

How many more points would he have had if he stayed rea-
sonably healthy? Four hundred? Five hundred? Six hundred?
We'll never know. No disrespect to Wayne Gretzky, Gordie
Howe, Mark Messier, Bobby Orr, Gilbert Perreault,…but
Mario did things nobody else could ever do.

–Bryan Trottier (1956–), New York Islanders center,
on Mario Lemieux

The first thing that pops into my mind is that he always
wore a tuque, a small, knitted hat with no brim in Montréal
colours—*bleu, blanc et rouge* [blue, white and red]. I also
remember him as the coolest man I ever saw, absolutely
imperturbable. He stood upright in the net and scarcely left
his feet; he simply played all his shots in a standing position.
Vézina was a pale, narrow-featured fellow, almost frail looking, yet remarkably good with his stick. He'd pick off more
shots with it than he did with his glove.

–Frank Boucher (1902–77), New York Rangers forward,
on goaltending legend Georges Vézina

I can't look excited because I'm not. I can't shout at other
players because that's not my style. I can't dive on easy shots
and make them look hard. I guess all I do is stop pucks.

–George Hainsworth (1895–1950), NHL Hall of Fame goaltender

I remember once in Ottawa he scored from center ice against
Clint Benedict. The puck was going so fast that Clint
couldn't move fast enough to get it.

–Aurel Joliat (1901–86), Montréal Canadiens left winger,
on Cecil "Babe" Dye

Babe had the most deadly shot in the NHL. He wasn't a really good skater, but the could blast that puck like dynamite and he was a terrific competitor. When I was with Ottawa, Coach Tommy Gorman would say to me, "King, if you check Dye tonight, and he fails to score, there'll be an extra 50 bucks in your paycheck." That's all I needed to hear. I'd check Babe like a hawk.

–Francis Michael "King" Clancy (1903–86), NHL player, coach and executive, on Toronto St. Pats legend Cecil "Babe" Dye

He doesn't play a game that draws a lot of attention to himself. But if you know the game of hockey, you just see that he never makes a mistake. I can count on one hand the amount of mistakes Nicklas Lidstrom has made in the six years I've been with him. He's unbelievable.

–Brendan Shanahan (1969–), New York Rangers forward, on his former Detroit Red wings teammate

I would pick Paddy Moran of Québec and Percy LeSueur of Ottawa for goal. In their heyday, Moran and LeSueur were two of the smartest goalers I ever saw in action.

–Lester Patrick (1883–1960), NHL player, coach and general manager, on pre-NHL goaltending greats Paddy Moran and Percy LeSueur

When Brimmy played with the Boston Bruins, he was in my opinion the best of the goaltenders, and that takes in a lot of territory. I thought he was better than Sawchuk.

–Milt Schmidt (1918–), Boston Bruins center, on teammate Frank Brimsek

I was ready to come here for so long, and I think I would have done well. I've dedicated my whole life to hockey, and I would have given playing in the NHL 150 percent.

–Vladislav Tretiak (1952–), Soviet Olympic goaltender, on not being allowed to play in the NHL

There was no description or category that fit Ken Dryden because what he did never happened before. How do you sum up a goalie that wins the Stanley Cup the season before he wins the Calder Trophy as Rookie of the Year?

–Larry Pleau (1947–), St. Louis Blues general manager, on former Montréal Canadiens teammate Ken Dryden

He was by far the best I ever saw. Bernie played 65 games a year, and there would only be a handful of bad performances. The rest weren't just good but great. Technically, he was the soundest of any goalie who ever played the game.

–Bobby Taylor (1945–), Philadelphia Flyers goaltender, on teammate Bernie Parent

Totally, and I mean totally, unpredictable.

–Ted Nolan (1958–), New York Islanders head coach, on how his former goaltender, Dominik Hašek, plays the game

He was a young guy from Montréal, like me. I idolized him because he came in to the NHL so young and he showed he could do the job. He made me see the possibility of doing it myself.

–Martin Brodeur (1972–), New Jersey Devils goaltender, on his boyhood hero, Montréal Canadiens goaltender Patrick Roy

GREATEST MOMENTS

Hockey is rife with great moments. But these great moments are brought to life by the words from players and coaches who were actually there to witness history.

I was sitting on the bench at the end of the final game, and I had a sense that I could get a goal. I needed to get out there to score a goal.

> –Paul Henderson (1943–), Team Canada left winger, remembering the moments before scoring the most famous goal in Canadian hockey history

Here's shot. Henderson made a wild stab for it and fell. Here's another shot, right in front—they score! Henderson scores for Canada! And the fans and the team are going wild! Henderson, right in front of the Soviet goal with 34 seconds left in the game!

> –Foster Hewitt (1902–85), Canadian hockey broadcaster, calling the last few moments of the final game of the Canada-USSR Summit Series, September 28, 1972, when Paul Henderson scored at 19:26 in the third period to win the series

I shot it again, and it went right along the ice, and I saw it go in the net. Holy Geez.

> –Paul Henderson (1943–), Team Canada left winger, to the media after scoring that winning goal

We want to win as many Stanley Cups as possible. I think we're one Cup away from being recognized as the greatest hockey team of all time.

> –Kevin Lowe (1959–), Edmonton Oilers defenseman, after winning the 1998 Stanley Cup

Nobody called me the "Jackie Robinson of hockey" then, but that's how I felt. Of course, Jackie had far worse things happen to him than I ever did, but there I was, in a place where no black man had ever been.

–Willie O'Ree (1935–), Boston Bruins right winger,
on being the first black player in the NHL

Seeing the famous photograph of me flying through the air after scoring the overtime goal to give the Boston Bruins the 1970 Stanley Cup brings back a flood of memories. I remember the thrill of getting that goal and the good fortune of being part of that special team. When I was a boy, I watched in awe as the Stanley Cup was carried high over the shoulders of the winning team, and today that photograph represents the excitement of realizing that dream.

–Bobby Orr (1948–), Boston Bruins defenseman, on scoring
the winning goal in the 1970 Stanley Cup finals against the
St. Louis Blues

I always tell Bobby he was up in the air for so long that I had time to shower and change before he hit the ice.

–Glenn Hall (1931–), St. Louis Blues goaltender,
on letting in Orr's goal

Wear your mask if you want, Jacques.

–Hector "Toe" Blake (1912–95), Montréal Canadiens head coach,
to goaltender Jacques Plante. Although Plante used the mask in
practice, Blake had refused to let him wear it in games. But in a
game on November 1, 1959, after only three minutes of play, a shot
hit Plante in the face and broke his nose, requiring stitches. There
was no backup goalie, and Plante refused to go back on without
the mask. Blake finally had to give in.

Plante was the happiest guy in the rink that he got cut. Don't ever feel sorry for him because he was looking for the opportunity.

–James Dickinson "Dick" Irvin Jr. (1932–), longtime Montréal
Canadiens broadcaster

The Detroit papers say we are finished. Hell, even the Toronto papers have written us off, but I ain't about to write us off.

–Clarence Henry "Hap" Day (1901–90), Toronto Maple Leafs head
coach, before Toronto rallied from a 3–0 series deficit to win the
1942 Stanley Cup finals

I heard a boom like a cannon. It was the bone cracking.

–Robert Neil "Bobby" Baun (1936–), Toronto Maple Leafs
defenseman, on breaking his leg in the 1964 Stanley Cup finals
and continuing to play

As much as the fans fault Reece for what happened, it was simply a night where every shot and pass I made seemed to pay off in a goal. I hit corners a couple of times, banking shots in off the post. The kid was screened on a couple of goals and had no chance. He didn't really flub one goal.

–Darryl Sittler (1950–),Toronto Maple Leafs center, on setting the
still-standing record for most points in a single game by scoring
6 goals and 4 assists on unlucky Boston Bruins goaltender Dave
Reece on February 7, 1976

To hit 76, I'd have to get 26 goals in 40 games. Never mind what's happened up 'til now, that's a lot of goals. I still have a long way to go, and I will not make any predictions. Now, if you guys will excuse me, I have to call my dad.

–Wayne Gretzky (1961–), NHL great, after scoring 50 goals in
39 games on December 30, 1981, and being asked by a reporter if he
would try to break Phil Esposito's record of 76 regular-season goals

I was going to number 66, whether he wanted it or not.

> —Wayne Gretzky (1961–), NHL great, on setting up the Team
> Canada's game-winning goal in the 1987 Canada Cup versus
> the Soviets

We tried our best not to let him break the record. We would never hear the end of it if he got that point against us. Don't believe that humble exterior. He loves to brag.

> —Kevin Lowe (1959–), Edmonton Oilers defenseman, on trying to
> prevent former Oiler Wayne Gretzky from scoring his 1851st point
> against his old team in 1989

You have always been the Great One, but tonight you are the Greatest.

> —Gary Bettman (1952–), NHL commissioner, to Wayne Gretzky
> after Gretzky broke Gordie Howe's record of 801 career goals,
> March 23, 1994

If you lose this game, you'll take it to your f***ing grave.

> —Herb Brooks (1937–2003), U.S. Olympic hockey coach,
> to the 1980 U.S. Olympic team before the gold-medal
> game versus Finland

I hear they had our flag on their dressing room floor. I wonder if they'd like us to sign it.

> —Hayley Wickenheiser (1978–), Canadian Olympic hockey player,
> in an emotional post-game CBC interview after defeating the
> U.S. women's team for the 2002 Winter Olympic gold medal

When the players first saw me at tryout, they were amused. But in no time they stopped treating me like a girl.

> —Manon Rhéaume (1972–), Canadian Olympic goaltender, on
> being the first female to play in the NHL, in an exhibition
> game for the Tampa Bay Lightning

I didn't enjoy that game very much. I had played only two previous NHL games, and seeing Dave in the other goal was a distraction I didn't want or need.

–Ken Dryden (1947–), NHL Hall of Fame goaltender, on playing goal against his brother Dave of the Buffalo Sabres

Win today, and we walk together forever.

–Fred Shero (1925–90), Philadelphia Flyers head coach, at the 1974 Stanley Cup finals

I can see them both there, and the pass goes practically to Mario's stick. He doesn't just not play it. He actually puts his stick there to play it, then moves his stick. It was a beautiful play, and a play you have to honor as a goalie. Obviously I honored it a bit too much.

–Mike Richter (1966–), U.S. Olympic goaltender, on Mario Lemieux's contribution to Canadian Paul Kariya's goal in the 2002 Olympic final, which tied the game 1–1

It was his last act of devotion to the club.

–Joseph Viateur "Leo" Dandurand (1889–1964), Montréal Canadiens owner, on goaltender Georges Vézina's last visit, in early 1926, to the see the team at the Mount Royal Arena to boost their morale before returning home, where he died of tuberculosis shortly afterward

Without being cocky, when it comes to overtime, we just feel we can win.

–Jacques Demers (1944–), former Montréal Canadiens head coach, on the Canadiens' incredible 10 straight overtime victories during their run to the Stanley Cup in the 1993 playoffs

INFAMOUS MOMENTS

As many famous moments as there are in hockey there are also infamous ones. From the tragedy of the 1919 Stanley Cup final influenza outbreak, through the Richard Riots of 1955, to Patrick Roy's last words as a member of the Montreal Canadiens, relive those moments that stop your heart.

All boys except Hall are doing nicely. Lalonde, Berlanquette, Couture have been normal for two days. They will get out Saturday. Kennedy has slight temperature yet, but consider him doing well and no danger. Hall developed pneumonia today he is easily worst case but we are hoping for the best. Have been here myself for three days and everything possible being done. Am leaving for Vancouver tonight.

–Frank A. Patrick (1885–1958), NHL head coach and hockey builder, in a telegram to NHL president Frank Calder from Seattle, Washington on April 3, 1919, commenting on the health of the Montréal Canadiens after they were stricken with the Spanish flu while in Seattle playing the Metropolitans for the Stanley Cup

I deserved a suspension of several games for shoving the lines-man during my fight with Hal Laycoe of the Bruins. I would have accepted that punishment if they had given it to me to serve, let's say, at the beginning of the following season, but not for the rest of the season and the playoffs. That suspen-sion removed all my chances of winning the scoring champi-onship, the most coveted title for a hockey player. For me, that was the most memorable moment of my career.

–Maurice Richard (1921–2000), Montréal Canadiens legend, on receiving what was, at the time, the longest suspension in NHL history, for a fight on March 13, 1955

He wouldn't listen. That's why I hit him.

> Maurice Richard (1921–2000), Montréal Canadiens legend, on
> why he punched out referee Cliff Thompson in that fight

It is my right and my duty to be present at the game both as a citizen and as president of the league, and if the mayor or Forum authorities had an apprehension they would not be able to deal with and had requested me to absent myself, I would gladly comply with their request.

> —Clarence Campbell (1905–84), NHL president, on his right to
> attend a game at the Montréal Forum after having suspended
> Maurice Richard for the rest of the season and the playoffs

What Campbell did was no more sensible than waving a red flag in front of an angry bull.

> —Maurice Richard (1921–2000), Montréal Canadiens legend, on
> Campbell's showing up at the Canadiens game four days after
> the suspension, which sparked the infamous Richard Riot on
> March 17, 1955

The people that come out of high school with the best grades go to the best universities. The people with the lower grades have fewer choices. Why should a player who comes out of junior hockey with top marks go to a city that is not his choice?

> —Eric Lindros (1973–), NHL center, on refusing to play for the
> Québec Nordiques after being selected by them in
> the 1991 NHL draft

He isn't black. He's a Bruin.

> —Milt Schmidt (1918–), Boston Bruins head coach, on Willie
> O'Ree, the first black NHL player

To the hockey palace his fame helped build and where he knew his greatest triumphs, the body of Howie Morenz was taken today for public services.

> –Headline from a Montréal newspaper, March 11, 1937,
> on the tragic death of Howie Morenz

Howie loved to play hockey more than anyone ever loved anything, and when he realized that he would never play again....Howie died of a broken heart.

> –Aurel Joliat (1901–86), Montréal Canadiens left winger,
> on former teammate Howie Morenz

I was the guy who killed him. I was stunned when I heard he'd died. I simply couldn't believe it. He was the greatest all-round player in the game.

> –Earl Siebert (1910–90), Chicago Blackhawks defenseman, on
> Howie Morenz. Seibert collided with Morenz unintentionally
> during a game on January 28, 1937, putting him in the hospi-
> tal with multiple fractures of his leg. Morenz died six weeks
> later of complications at the age of 34. Seibert never forgave
> himself for what happened and lived the rest of his life regret-
> ting that day on the ice.

What I find interesting is that 200 people died in terrorist bombings in Spain, and the biggest news story across Canada was Todd Bertuzzi. I think we need to get our priorities set straight as to what's really important in life.

> –Dave "Tiger" Williams (1954–), NHL enforcer, on the March 8,
> 2004, incident where Vancouver Canucks right winger Todd
> Bertuzzi punched Colorado Avalanche center Steve Moore in the
> head from behind, knocking him out and causing him to fall
> hard on the ice. Moore sustained a severe concussion and several
> fractured vertebrae and was ultimately forced to retire from
> professional hockey as a consequence.

Mr. Bertuzzi pursued Mr. Moore on the ice, attempting to engage him in a confrontation. When Mr. Moore declined to engage Mr. Bertuzzi, Mr. Bertuzzi responded by delivering a gloved punch from behind to the side of Mr. Moore's head, rendering him unconscious. Upon falling to the ice, Mr. Moore suffered additional serious injuries. We want to make clear that this type of conduct will not be tolerated in the NHL.

—Colin Campbell (1953–), NHL vice-president, announcing Todd Bertuzzi's suspension

Steve, I just want to apologize for what happened out there. I had no intention of hurting you.

—Todd Bertuzzi (1975–), Vancouver Canucks right winger, apologizing tearfully to Steve Moore

I can't explain how scary it is.

—Steve Moore (1978–), Colorado Avalanche forward, speaking three weeks after the attack

Looks worse than it is, though, right? I've just got to wear this stylish brace for a while.

—Steve Moore (1978–), Colorado Avalanche forward, on his neck brace

It's the hardest thing I've ever been through. I don't think there's an August 9 where I haven't thought about it.

—Wayne Gretzky (1961–), NHL great, on the trade that sent him from the Edmonton Oilers to the Los Angeles Kings in 1988

He came down again, and I got my elbows up and roughed him, which he didn't take kindly to. So we dropped the gloves and started flailing away at each other. Then, to my amazement, I felt something soft. I had a full head of hair in my hands! I looked down and discovered I was holding Bobby's wig. I said, "Oh, sh**! and threw the hairpiece out in the middle of the ice. Bobby just stood there completely bald, and the fans were as stunned as he was. It was as if the air had been sucked out of the building.

> —Dave Hanson (1954–), NHL defenseman, on removing Bobby Hull's hairpiece during a WHA game

After all these years in the league, am I that stupid that I would put four forwards and one defenseman in a 3–3 tie, in the third period? I think everybody that knows me here knows I'm not that stupid. I might be halfway stupid, but not that stupid.

> —Pat Burns (1952–), New Jersey Devils head coach, after referees negated a line change that led to Tampa Bay's winning goal in game three of the Eastern Conference semifinal in the 2002 Stanley Cup playoffs

Most of the guys that wear them are Europeans and French guys.

> —Don Cherry (1934–), Canadian hockey commentator, on hockey visors, a comment that caused a national uproar

To understand the feelings of the crowd that night is to understand a good bit of the social conditions of Québec of the 1950s.

> —Hugh MacLennan (1907–90), Canadian writer, on the 1955 Richard Riots

I felt disgusted with myself for letting it happen. Sometimes when you have too many men on the ice it's the player's fault. But not this time. I hadn't spelled out the assignments plainly enough.

–Don Cherry (1934–), Canadian hockey commentator, when he was head coach of the Boston Bruins, on the penalty during the 1979 playoffs in the final game of the series between the Bruins and the Montréal Canadiens that allowed the Canadiens to tie the score and send the game into overtime, where the Canadiens won

I don't believe in winning that way!

–Barry Melrose (1956–), Los Angeles Kings head coach, on Montréal Canadiens head coach Jacques Demers's call on Marty McSorley's illegal curved stick during the 1993 Stanley Cup finals

That's the last time I played for Montréal.

–Patrick Roy (1965–), Montréal Canadiens goaltender, to Canadiens President Ronald Corey, after being pulled in an embarrassing 9–1 loss against the Detroit Red Wings on December 2, 1995

I was never the type of man to hold grudges against anybody.

–Irvine Wallace "Ace" Bailey (1903–92), former Toronto Maple Leafs right winger, to reporters on shaking hands with Eddie Shore at an all-star benefit game at Maple Leaf Gardens. Shore was the man who had checked Bailey on December 12, 1933, causing the injury that ended Bailey's career.

THOSE OUTSIDE THE GAME

While hockey is not as popular as baseball or football, the sport has still managed to make an impression on people outside of the game. From comedians to actors, everyone seems to have an opinion about the game.

I went to a fight the other night, and a hockey game broke out.

–Rodney Dangerfield (1921–2004), American comedian

This is the only thing that has seen more parties than us.

–Steven Tyler (1948–), lead singer for Aerosmith, after admiring the Stanley Cup

I had all my own teeth, and I wanted to keep it that way.

–Tom Glavine (1966–), Major League Baseball pitcher, on why he played baseball rather than hockey

Why, it looks just like the gondola on an airship.

–C.M. Passmore, executive with MacLaren Advertising Limited, when shown the broadcasting booth among the rafters at Maple Leaf Gardens in 1931

Americans could never, will never and cannot understand Shakespeare. They're far more fascinated with Cabbage Patch Dolls, the Hula Hoop and the local hockey team, which is largely made up of Canadians. That's the best joke of all.

–Marlon Brando (1924–2004), American actor, while filming in Toronto in 1989

There'll be fresh blood on the ice this year.

> –Dave Broadfoot (1925–), Canadian comedian

Bobby Orr has been to Boston the equivalent of a great natural or historic resource, like Paul Revere's house or the Bunker Hill monument.

> –Kevin White (1929–), mayor of Boston, when Bobby Orr left Boston to play for the Chicago Blackhawks in 1976

It's not a sport you get famous at. If I wanted to be famous, I would have stuck with hockey.

> –Eric Heiden (1958–), American Olympic speed skater, speaking about his sport

Why don't you make like a hockey player and get the puck out of here?

> –Charlie Sheen (1965–), American actor

I was thrilled one year when I was younger when not only did my brothers get hockey sticks for Christmas—but I did too!

> –Nancy Kerrigan (1969–), American Olympic figure skater

I always wanted to play hockey, and my parents wouldn't let me. I swear, they're not bad parents; they just wanted to protect me.

> –Maria Menounos (1978–), American actress

Basketball isn't as popular in Canada as it is in the U.S. Hockey is by far the most popular sport in Canada.

> –Steve Nash (1974–), Phoenix Suns point guard

Hockey is a sport for white men. Basketball is a sport for black men. Golf is a sport for white men dressed like black pimps.

–Tiger Woods (1975–), professional golfer

I am like the Jack Nicholson of the [Los Angeles] Kings— every single game. If there was a game tonight I wouldn't be here. I used to play hockey. That was my original thing. My first thing, I wanted to play professional hockey.

–Rob Zombie (1966–), heavy metal musician and movie director, comparing his devotion to the Kings to Nicholson's devotion to the Los Angeles Lakers basketball team

Hockey captures the essence of Canadian experience in the New World. In a land so inescapably and inhospitably cold, hockey is the chance of life, and an affirmation that despite the deathly chill of winter we are alive.

–Stephen Leacock (1869–1944), Canadian writer

I'm as much of a collector, a lover of old hockey as the next guy. This is about sharing the piece with fans around the world.

–Brian Price, businessman, on his plans to shred the only existing pair of goalie pads of George Vézina and affix the pieces to hockey cards

I'm not planning a career change—not unless they need someone who constantly falls on the ice and is out of breath all the time.

–Scott Wolf (1968–), American actor, after playing in a charity hockey game

The hockey lockout of 1994–95 has been settled. They have stopped bickering…and can now get down to some serious bloodshed.

–Conan O'Brien (1963–), host of *Late Night with Conan O'Brien*

A puck is a hard rubber disc that hockey players strike when they can't hit one another.

–Jimmy Cannon (1910–73), American sports journalist

Ice hockey is a form of disorderly conduct in which the score is kept.

–Doug Larson (1902–81), English automobile racer

They handled me like a sack of potatoes. Of course, they told me Leach was a psychological ruin after he failed to beat me. And they said I'd made 30 or 40 saves at least in my brief appearance.

–George Plimpton (1927–2003), American journalist, on becoming an NHL goaltender for a few minutes in the fall of 1977 during the pre-season with the Boston Bruins

Playing hockey, there were a lot of guys bigger than me, so I knew I was going to get hit and have to deal with it. You gotta hit back.

–Mike Weir (1970–), Canadian professional golfer

Black people dominate sports in the United States. Twenty percent of the population and 90 percent of the Final Four [college basketball]. We own this sh**. Basketball, baseball, football, golf, tennis, and as soon as they make a heated hockey rink we'll take that sh** too.

–Chris Rock (1965–), American comedian

I love Canada, with the hockey games and the f***in' spirit—everybody gets so f***in' into it.

–Neil Young (1945–), singer, quoted in his biography, *Shakey*, by Jimmy McDonough

Mario Lemieux is Mr. Pittsburgh.

–Andy Van Slyke (1960–), Pittsburgh Pirates center fielder

The place was always cold, and I got the feeling that the fans would have enjoyed baseball more if it had been played with a hockey puck.

–Andre Dawson (1954–), Montréal Expos outfielder, on playing baseball in front of Canadians

It's so quick and so brutal, and I'm just in shock. I'm amazed that people don't keep screaming 911!

–Robin Williams (1951–), American comedian, on hockey

My name is Happy Gilmore. Ever since I was old enough to skate, I loved hockey. Wasn't really the greatest skater though, but that didn't stop my dad from teaching me the secret of his greatest slap shot.

–Adam Sandler (1966–), American actor, from the movie *Happy Gilmore*

During high school, I played junior hockey and still hold two league records: most time spent in the penalty box; and I was the only guy to ever take off his skate and try to stab somebody.

–Adam Sandler (1966–), American actor, from the movie *Happy Gilmore*

SIDNEY CROSBY

Not since Wayne Gretzky or Mario Lemieux has one player electrified the imaginations and passions of so many as Sidney Crosby. Although just a few years into his NHL career, the young star has broken away from the comparisons to the former greats and has started to clear a space for himself in the history books.

I'm not trying to be the next Wayne Gretzky or Mario Lemieux,…I am putting pressure on myself to do my best and perform to my potential—that's all I can do.

—Sidney Crosby (1987–), Pittsburgh Penguins center

It means a lot to us, to the league and to Rimouski. We are very proud to have him in our league.

—Gilles Courteau, Québec Major Junior Hockey League commissioner, on Sidney Crosby's signing with the QMJHL Rimouski Océanic in 2003

I don't think there's ever a time where I step back and say I wish I was something different. I'm doing what I love to do.

—Sidney Crosby (1987–), Pittsburgh Penguins center

I'd love to have the opportunity to do that.…Obviously I'm going to be a rookie, so I'm going to try to learn as much as I can, be open-minded. And be a student…I'm going to learn from one of the best guys in Mario Lemieux. So I'm going to try and be a sponge in that way and learn as much as I can from him.

—Sidney Crosby (1987–), Pittsburgh Penguins center, on getting to learn from the Pittsburgh Penguins' greatest player in his rookie year

I looked forward to it for a long time. It feels awesome. Yeah, I was happy. It's something you dream of, scoring in the NHL, and you only do it the first time once. It was big. There's a lot of emotion. The fans were great. It was so loud. I never expected to hear them [chanting] my name. You never expect that.

—Sidney Crosby (1987–), Pittsburgh Penguins center

I realize there will not be another Gretzky, and I will be the first one to say I will not break his records....But for him to say that I could, it means I am doing something right. It was probably the best compliment I could get. I'm going to remember it.

—Sidney Crosby (1987–), Pittsburgh Penguins center

My dad introduced me to the game, gave me a stick. Since then I've had a passion for it.

—Sidney Crosby (1987–), Pittsburgh Penguins center

You can see the talent is there. I don't know if you got a true vision of him tonight. It's tough to play your first NHL game.

—Larry Robinson (1951–), New Jersey Devils coach, on watching Sidney Crosby's performance against the Devils in Crosby's first game in the NHL, October 5, 2005

I haven't changed one bit. I never dove, and I don't dive now.... That's just part of the playoffs, part of gamesmanship. If I go down, it's because I've been forced down. I'll do whatever I can to stay on my feet. I think he [Renney] should be the one worried about diving.

—Sidney Crosby (1987–), Pittsburgh Penguins center, on accusations by New York Rangers head coach Tom Renney that he was taking dives during the 2008 Stanley Cup playoffs Eastern Conference semifinal

I want to be the best. So whatever comes with that, I have to accept it.

—Sidney Crosby (1987–), Pittsburgh Penguins center

Crosby, in large part because his father Troy was drafted by the team, was always a big Montréal Canadiens fan. Prior to the 2005 entry draft it was widely assumed he would have liked to have been drafted by the Canadiens. Now 19, Crosby will be eligible for free agency when he turns 25, at which point he can sign with any team. He has never come right out and said it specifically, but I have no doubt in my mind that he would one day like to play for the Montréal Canadiens. I think it would mean a lot to him. I think he has a lot of love for the city of Montréal.

—Shawna Richer, author, in her book *The Kid: A Season with Sidney Crosby and the New NHL*

I think he has a moat around his house with a dragon guarding the front gate. The guy is a legend. He's the only guy in the world with a dragon. I think Tim Horton's hired a dragon to guard him.

—Colby Armstrong (1982–), Atlanta Thrashers right winger, on former Pittsburgh Penguins teammate Sidney Crosby

I want to make the world juniors team and play against a lot of world-class teams. It was heart breaking last year, and I definitely want to do it again.

—Sidney Crosby (1987–), Pittsburgh Penguins center, on his experiences at the World Junior Hockey Championship tournaments

No special treatment at home. He has a little sister he has to fight over the TV with.

—Troy Crosby (1966–), father of Sidney, on his son's rise to fame

Being Canadian, you want to play for Team Canada. With the talent that Canada has, they always have a chance to win. It would be nice to be part of that.

—Sidney Crosby (1987–), Pittsburgh Penguins center, on participating in the 2010 Olympics

It's hard to compare, because you look at his size, there were players of his size [in the past]. But work like he works, they will not.

—Jacques Lemaire (1945–), Minnesota Wild coach, on Sidney Crosby's potential for greatness, while using the grammar of Master Yoda

Our savior has arrived.

—Sign held by unidentified Pittsburgh Penguins fan during Sidney Crosby's first season with the Penguins in 2005

I have been practicing since I was four or five years old, but that wasn't really practice. I was just having fun. I just loved to play hockey.

—Sidney Crosby (1987–), Pittsburgh Penguins center

For every whack I've given, I've gotten four or five.

—Sidney Crosby (1987–), Pittsburgh Penguins center

It's not that hard to stay grounded. It's the way I was brought up.

—Sidney Crosby (1987–), Pittsburgh Penguins center, on responding to pressure

I need to work on defensive play and being consistent.

—Sidney Crosby (1987–), Pittsburgh Penguins center, on the aspects of his game that need improvement

I didn't anticipate anything—I was just showing up and seeing what the town and people were about, but it was a very welcoming sight....I'm sure the energy and excitement in town are going to rub off on the players. It's nice to see everybody's so excited about getting hockey started.

—Sidney Crosby (1987–), Pittsburgh Penguins center

He keeps you on the edge of your seat. He gets off the ice, and you can't wait to see him get back on.

—Gilles Meloche (1950–), Pittsburgh Penguins goaltending coach and former NHL player, on Sidney Crosby

He said he needs to work on his shot a little bit, but it looks pretty good to me.

—Mario Lemieux (1965–), Pittsburgh Penguins great

I've won the Stanley Cup, won gold medals. Getting Sidney Crosby was the happiest day of my life.

—Craig Patrick (1946–), Pittsburgh Penguins executive, on winning the draft lottery and selecting Sidney Crosby

You're not going to intimidate this kid. He's not going to back off. There are players like that. When we played against Henri Richard or Frank Mahovlich, the word at our meetings was to leave those guys alone. Ask them how their families are doing, but don't wake them up. If you tick them off, they become even better players.

—Ed Johnston (1935–), Pittsburgh Penguins executive and former NHL player

We have a very strong idea of being grounded. We understand the real world and how it works.

—Trina Crosby, Sidney's mother

IT'S A CANADIAN GAME

Hockey is and always will be a Canadian game. It was brought to life on the ponds and rinks of this great nation and has made its mark on our culture and traditions.

In English-speaking Canada, hockey sometimes seems to be the sole assurance that we have a culture. That is something never in question in Québec.

–Rick Salutin (1942–), Canadian writer, in the preface to his play
Les Canadiens

Canadian professional hockey is proud and touchy. Canada is the birthplace of this tremendous game. You invented it, and you always want to be the best.

–Anatoli Tarasov (1918–95), CSKA Moscow and USSR national
hockey coach

The Canadian player must please the spectators with his individual ability while his Soviet opposite concentrates his efforts on a team victory.

–Anatoli Tarasov (1918–95), CSKA Moscow and USSR national
hockey coach

There is pictorial evidence of a hockey-like game (Kalv) being played on the ice in The Netherlands in the early 16th Century. The game probably was first played in North America on December 25, 1855, at Kingston, Ontario, Canada, but Halifax also lays claim to priority.

–David A. Boehm (1914–2000), editor of the
Guinness Sports Record Book

This is the only country in the world where, in thousands of gardens, tomato plants are held up with broken hockey sticks. This is a unique Canadian happening.

–Robert F. Harney (1939–89), director of the Multicultural
History Society of Ontario

Hockey is Canada's game. It may also be Canada's national theatre. On its frozen stage, each night the stuff of life is played out: ambition, hope, pride, fear, love and friendship, the fight for honor for city, team, each other, and themselves. The puck flips one way, bounces another, and the player set out to control and direct it. It takes them where they never planned to go. It tests them. And in struggling to get it back, with the millions who watch in the arena or by television, the players find out who they really are. Like the bear pits in Shakespeare's time, we attend hockey games as our national theatre. It is a place where the monumental themes of Canadian life are played out—English and French, East and West, Canada and the U.S., Canada and the world, the timeless tensions of commerce and culture, our struggle to survive and civilize winter.

–Roy MacGregor (1948–), Canadian writer, and Ken Dryden
(1947–), NHL Hall of Fame goaltender, from their book
Home Game

Hockey is our winter ballet and in many ways our own national theatre.

–Morley Callaghan (1903–90), Canadian writer

Canada is hockey!

–Mike Weir (1970–), Canadian professional golfer

The Canadians were the inventors of the body check, the penalty bench, and the widespread view of fans that athletes who shirk bodily contact are pansies.

–Karl Adolf Scherer, European hockey historian

Canada is made up of half-failed hockey players—and half women—all of us involved in a shared delusion, whether in a church league in Toronto or the Wild Goose League in Saskatchewan.

–Dick Beddoes (1926–91), Canadian sportswriter

Canadians can't play baseball because baseball is a summer game, and Canada has no summer. Canadians should stick to their native sports, namely, hockey and pelt trapping.

–Jimmy Breslin (1930–), American writer, commenting on singer Mary O'Dowd's forgetting the words to the U.S. national anthem at a Toronto Blue Jays–New York Yankees game

We have to put a stop to this. We have to find out who these aliens are who dropped in on us with these bylaws and step on them. Squash them like a bug.

–Dave "Tiger" Williams (1954–), Toronto Maple Leafs defenseman, on the bylaws in some Canadian cities banning street hockey games

I would sometimes imagine one great outdoor hockey game, stretching from just inside the Rockies to the shores of the Atlantic, detouring only around the too temperate climates of a few of the bigger cities.

–Peter Gzowski (1934–2002), Canadian writer and broadcaster, on hockey in Canada

Most young Canadians…are born with skates on their feet rather than with silver spoons in their mouths.

–Lester B. Pearson (1897–1972), Canadian prime minister

You ever try carrying an anvil on your back for 10 days?

–Al MacInnis (1963–), NHL defenseman and Team Canada member, when asked about the pressure on Canada's Olympic hockey team to win gold

ON WAYNE GRETZKY

*Simply the greatest player to put on a pair of skates, so a lot
of people had things to say about the Great One.*

You miss 100 percent of the shots you never take.

—Wayne Gretzky (1961–), NHL great

Some guys play hockey. Gretzky plays 40 mph chess.

—Lowell Cohn, American sportswriter

We're the only show in town. Coming to see Gretzky is like
going to watch Pavarotti or Nureyev. What else are you going
to do in Edmonton in the middle of winter? How many beers
can you drink?

—Peter Pocklington (1943–), Edmonton Oilers owner, when asked
by journalist Mordecai Richler, if the NHL season is long enough.

Gretzky is something else again....He strikes me as the first
nondescript hockey star. Sometimes you don't even realize
he's out there, watching as he whirls, until he emerges out
of nowhere, finding open ice, and accelerating to a score....
Watching him out there, I've often felt he's made of
Plasticine....Gretzky is arguably the best player hockey has
ever known.

—Mordecai Richler (1931–2001), Canadian writer

Dear Mr. Wayne Gretzky, Would it be possible to set up an
appointment to see you? Signed, Your Father.

—Walter Gretzky (1938–), in a letter sent to his son Wayne during
the 1981–82 playoffs

Practice your backhand.

> —Gordie Howe (1928–), Detroit Red Wings great, giving advice to
> young hockey hopeful Wayne Gretzky, then only eleven

Gordie was saying something the other day that is true.
The hardest thing about hockey is that the older you get, the
more you love it. I've said many times that I enjoy it more
now than when I was 19, when I first came in. I think part
of the reason is that you know you're getting closer to the
end. I love the game now more than ever.

> —Wayne Gretzky (1961–), NHL great

Hey, you're not the greatest! I am the greatest! They call you
The Great One, but only I am the greatest!

> —Muhammad Ali (1942–), heavyweight boxing champion,
> to Wayne Gretzky

No argument here, sir.

> —Wayne Gretzky (1961–), NHL great, replying to Muhammed Ali

Wayne will get at least 3000 points before he's finished.
When he's through, his record will last for a long time.

> —Gordie Howe (1928–), Detroit Red Wings great. Howe was pre-
> scient: Gretzky finished his NHL playing career with 3239 points
> (2857 in the regular season, 382 in playoffs).

I feel I've gained more than I lost. I lost a record, but I gained
a lot of friends.

> —Gordie Howe (1928–), Detroit Red Wings great, after Wayne
> Gretzky broke his career scoring record of 1850 goals

They will think I'm crazy buying a lawn sprinkler in
February.

> –Phyllis Gretzky (1941–2005), when husband Walter asked her to
> buy a replacement sprinkler to finish the backyard rink for their son

He is hockey now. Although virtually every age of the game
has had its pre-eminent players—Morenz, Richard, Howe,
Hull, Orr—no one has ever transcended it as he has. An
American magazine that once used to treat hockey with little
more seriousness than steeplechasing has called him "the
greatest athlete in the world." A newspaper piece I read last
weekend on the news of his engagement made reference to
Charles and Di. The little kid from Brantford is now the biggest star we have.

> –Peter Gzowski (1934–2002), Canadian writer and broadcaster,
> in a 1988 *Maclean's* article on Wayne Gretzky

I remember when he got off that little jet I sent to get him.
Here's this skinny kid with peach fuzz. I thought, "My God,
I paid $750,000 for that?" Just kidding.

> –Peter Pocklington (1943–), owner of the Edmonton Oilers,
> on hiring Wayne Gretzky

My fondest memory of Wayne is undoubtedly the Canada
Cup. Practicing with him and playing alongside Wayne for
six weeks was the turning point in my career. He showed me
how to win, and for that I am eternally grateful.

> –Mario Lemieux (1965–), Pittsburgh Penguins great,
> on Gretzky's retirement from the NHL

The hardest thing for me has always been that I've been compared to myself.

> –Wayne Gretzky (1961–), NHL great

You'll never catch me bragging about goals, but I'll talk all you want about my assists.

—Wayne Gretzky (1961–), NHL great

The only way you can check Gretzky is to hit him when he is standing still singing the national anthem.

—Harry Sinden (1932–), Boston Bruins general manager

Parents come up to me now saying, "We'd like you to tell our son that he has to practice hockey the way you did, for six, seven or eight hours a day." I tell them that's not my philosophy. It really wasn't practice, it was fun. I enjoyed myself. If I had considered it practice, I would not have done it.

—Wayne Gretzky (1961–), NHL great

The next time you see me skating, it'll be with my kids.

—Wayne Gretzky (1961–), NHL great, on his retirement

Procrastination is one of the most common and deadliest of diseases, and its toll on success and happiness is heavy.

—Wayne Gretzky, (1961–), NHL great

I had to play the same style all the way through. I couldn't beat people with my strength. I don't have a hard shot. I'm not the quickest skater in the league. My eyes and my mind had to do most of the work.

—Wayne Gretzky (1961–), NHL great

I'm hoping for a bench-clearing brawl during the warm-up so I can go out and grab his stick.

—Ron Tugnutt (1967–), Ottawa Senators goaltender, on Gretzky's last game in Canada, which was against the Senators

When you take off that sweater, your jersey, after today's game, you will be the last player in the NHL to ever wear 99. You have always been and you will always be "The Great One," and there will never be another.

–Gary Bettman (1952–), NHL commissioner, at the retirement of
Gretzky's number 99 league-wide

By far Gretzky is the most talented player ever. Every time he gets the puck something exciting happens.

–Mike Milbury (1952–), New York Islanders general manager

The NHL needs something to hang its hat on, and Gretzky looks like a hat tree.

–Gordie Howe (1928–), Detroit Red Wings great

Gretzky would dominate in any era. It doesn't make any difference. He may well be the smartest hockey player who ever played the game.

–Phil Esposito (1942–), Boston Bruins great

ON GOALIES

It is amazing that a human being would willingly place themselves in front of a frozen piece of vulcanized rubber traveling at blistering speeds, but there seems to be an inexhaustible number of hockey players happy to jump in front of the net with a few pads on in order to stop that little puck. They are called goaltenders, and they are some of the strangest ones on the ice.

I just made up my mind that I was going to lose my teeth and have my face cut to pieces.

> –Johnny Bower (1924–), Toronto Maple Leafs goaltender, when asked how he decided to become a goalie.

After all, the only thing a goaltender has is his eyes.

> –Cecil R. "Tiny" Thompson (1905–81), Boston Bruins goaltender, on not reading in order to keep his eyes fresh

There is no position in sport as noble as goaltending.

> –Vladislav Tretiak (1952–), Soviet Olympic goalie

He's so cool, playoff pressure merely brings him up to normal.

> –Conn Symthe (1895–1980), Toronto Maple Leafs owner and hockey builder, on Turk Broda, the portly Toronto Maple Leafs goaltender from the 1940s.

Broda hasn't a nerve in his body. He could tend goal in a tornado and never blink an eye!

> –Jack Adams (1895–1968), Detroit Red Wings coach and general manager

The posts were my friends, so I just said hello to them. If I missed a shot, maybe it would hit them and stay out of the net.

–Patrick Roy (1965–), Montréal Canadiens goaltender, when asked if it was true that he talked to his goal posts

How would you like it if, at your job, every time you made the slightest mistake a little red light went on over your head and 18,000 people stood up and screamed at you?

–Jacques Plante (1929–86), Montréal Canadiens Hall of Fame goaltender

I play a position where you make mistakes. The only people who don't make them at a hockey game are the ones watching.

–Patrick Roy (1965–), Montréal Canadiens goaltender

Sometimes when I make a good save I yell out, "Woo-Hoo!" I'm not sure why, but it just feels good. I don't think I scare anyone or freak anyone out when I do it. I just like to holler when I make a tough stop.

–Marc-André Fleury (1984–), Pittsburgh Penguins goaltender

That 100-foot skate to the bench after you have been pulled is the longest, slowest skate in the world. It seems like five miles.

–Kelly Hrudey (1961–), Los Angeles Kings goaltender

Anyone who wears one is chicken. My face is my mask.

–Lorne "Gump" Worsley (1929–2007), Montréal Canadiens goaltender

My style? What do you mean my style? My style is to stop pucks!

–Roman Čechmánek (1971–), Philadelphia Flyers goaltender

Because the demands on a goalie are mostly mental, it means that for a goalie, the biggest enemy is himself. Not a puck, not an opponent, not a quirk or size or style. Him.

–Ken Dryden (1947–), Montréal Canadiens Hall of Fame goaltender

It's pretty tough for a goalie when you look at it. You're always the last line of defense. If you let a goal in, you can't go to the bench and hide between the guys or anything.

–Kirk McLean (1966–), Vancouver Canucks goaltender

There's only one job in sports that's worse and that would be as the javelin catcher on a track team.

–Lorne "Gump" Worsley (1929–2007),
Montréal Canadiens goaltender

I got sick of being hit in the face with pucks, especially deflected slapshots, so I wore a mask. Management opposed it and felt it showed I had lost my nerve. But it wasn't their faces that were being stitched all the time. It didn't take a genius to figure out that a mask could stop the stitches.

–Jacques Plante (1929–86), Montréal Canadiens goaltender,
on his reason for wearing a mask

If they let me wear it all the time, I can play until I'm 45.

–Jacques Plante (1929–86), Montréal Canadiens goaltender,
on wearing his new mask

Playing goal is like being shot at.

–Jacques Plante (1929–86), Montréal Canadiens goaltender

I'm not dumb enough to be a goalie.

–Brett Hull (1964–), Detroit Red Wings right winger

Goaltenders are three sandwiches shy of a picnic. From the moment primitive man lurched erect, he survived on the principle that when something hard and potentially lethal comes toward you at great velocity, get the hell out of its path.

—Jim Taylor, sports journalist

With goaltenders, when they are on, the pucks look like beach balls. When they are a little bit off, they look like BBs.

—Barry Trotz (1962–), Nashville Predators head coach

Terry Sawchuk is the greatest goaltender ever. He was the kind of player who only went through the motions in practice and warm-up but, come game time, there was none better. One of Terry's strengths was his crouch—it was one of the best that I'd ever witnessed. He remained square to the shooter as much as possible but cheated on rushes in that he wasn't the quickest goalie to come out and cut down the angle. But his cat-like reflexes were what allowed him to stay a little deeper in the net.

—Johnny Bower (1924–), Toronto Maple Leafs goaltender

I figure I only have so many saves left in me, and I want to save them for the games.

—Terry Sawchuk (1929–70), Detroit Red Wings goaltender, on why he never worked hard during practice

The tension was overwhelming, and the fans were screaming, "Roouu-ah, Roouu-ah." It got me off to a good start in the NHL.

—Patrick Roy (1965–), Montréal Canadiens goaltender, on the 1986 playoffs, during his rookie year

Roy's feat isn't something you can accomplish by having a good season. This is something you only accomplish by having years of good seasons, over a lifetime of playing. When you also take into account that he did it in 121 fewer games than Terry Sawchuk, to say he has had a truly outstanding career doesn't say it well enough.

> –Gary Bettman (1952–), NHL commissioner, on Patrick Roy eclipsing Terry Sawchuk's career record of 447 wins

Here kid, take care of this place until I get back.

> –Clint Benedict (1894–1976), Ottawa Senators goaltender, to a young "King" Clancy when skating off the ice to serve a penalty during a Stanley Cup playoff game on March 31, 1923. Clancy, normally a defenseman, played goal for the two minutes Benedict was off, thereby becoming the first and only person to play all six positions during a single game.

If you jump out of a plane without a parachute, does that make you brave? No, I think that makes you stupid. I will never play without a mask again.

> –Jacques Plante (1929–86), Montréal Canadiens goaltender

Our first priority was staying alive. Our second was stopping the puck.

> –Glenn Hall (1931–), Detroit Red Wings goaltender, on being a goalie in the NHL

I am not afraid to stop the puck with my head. I try to do it sometimes even in practice; not everyday, but once in a while. I say to my teammates, shoot me in the head, and I'll try to stop the puck. I am not afraid at all of the puck, so sometimes, if the shot comes at my head, it's an easier save to make with your head. Maybe the people think a different way, but for me, I do it with my head.

> –Dominik Hašek (1965–), Detroit Red Wings goaltender

My goalie's too fat. He'd better lose seven pounds before the next game, or I'll be looking for another goalie.

—Conn Symthe (1895–1980), Toronto Maple Leafs owner and hockey builder, on a slightly overweight Turk Broda

It may be safer facing Nazi U-boats in the Atlantic than dodging hockey pucks in the NHL.

—Sam LoPresti (1917–84), Chicago Blackhawks goaltender

I don't mind having a four-goals-against average if everybody does.

—Tomáš Vokoun (1976–), Florida Panthers goaltender

A big part of it is, the goalies are the best players on every team now. That's slowly evolved over the past 10 years. They're the superstars of the league and the highest-paid players, and they're the TV announcers. They practically run the league. Is that what you want in your sport? When I was growing up, your best athletes were your top centers and your top defensemen and the guys who played all the time. That's the way it should be in the NHL again.

—James Patrick (1963–), Buffalo Sabres defenseman

I don't think. I've told you guys before, goalies don't think.

—Chris Osgood (1972–), Detroit Red Wings goaltender, on facing Wayne Gretzky coming in on a breakaway

Steady strain. That is the fate of us goaltenders.

—Jacques Plante (1929–86), Hall of Fame goaltender, to a young Vladislav Tretiak

I was trying to get out of practice one day when this shot that couldn't have broken an egg hit me in the mask. I faked a serious injury and went into the dressing room. I was sitting there having a Coke when [Bruins coach] Harry Sinden came in and told me to get back out onto the ice. All the guys were laughing, so I knew I had to do something. I told the trainer to paint a 30-stitch gash on the mask. Then I went out and told Harry, "See how bad it is!?"

—Gerry Cheevers (1940–), Boston Bruins goaltender, on how he began painting stitches on his mask

If there is a comparison to an NHL goalie I would make for Tretiak, it would be Terry Sawchuk.

—Paul Henderson (1943–), Toronto Maple Leafs left winger, on Soviet goaltender Vladislav Tretiak

SCORING

*The whole point of the game is to score goals. These are
some of the greatest scorers and the greatest goals.*

Over the years, people have asked me whether it was true that
I actually scored a goal while carrying an opponent on my
back, and the answer is yes.

–Maurice Richard, (1921–2000), Montréal Canadiens great, on the
goal in which he carried big Detroit Red Wings defenseman Earl
Siebert on his back from the blue line and scored a goal

Listen, Mr. Adams. I weigh over 200 pounds. Any guy who
can carry me on his back from the blue line to the net
deserves to score a goal.

–Earl Siebert (1910–90), Detroit Red Wings defenseman,
to Detroit coach Jack Adams on why he didn't stop
Maurice Richard from scoring

Shades of Mario.

–John Vanbiesbrouck (1963–), New Jersey Devils goaltender, on
a particularly elegant goal by Pittsburgh Penguins center Evgeni
Malkin against the Devils

I have no sympathy for goalies. No sympathy at all. My job
is to go out there and score goals, and their job is to try and
stop me.

–Mario Lemieux (1965–), Pittsburgh Penguins great

His shot is like a piece of lead. You have to see it coming
toward you to believe it.

–Jacques Plante (1929–86), Hall of Fame goaltender

I'm going to look for opportunities to grab the puck by the hair and try to do something with it. I mean, it's not like I have to save the whole country with it. I just have to put it in the net.

—Sergei Fedorov (1969–), Detroit Red Wings center

If you want money, go to the bank. If you want bread, go to the bakery. If you want goals, go to the net.

—Brooks Laich (1983–), Washington Capitals center, on the key to his recent goal-scoring prowess

Hole in one! Hey guys I got a hole-in-one! I swear!

—Alexander Ovechkin (1985–), Washington Capitals left winger, after getting a hole-in-one during a team golf event before starting his rookie season

My buddy sent me a YouTube video today of [Pavel] Bure in the [1998 Winter] Olympics when he scored five goals against Finland.

—Marian Gaborik (1982–), Minnesota Wild right winger from Slovakia, on the inspiration behind his five-goal outburst in a 6–3 win over the New York Rangers on December 20, 2007

In that final game with Vancouver, Glen Sather wanted to keep the score down, win the game, and avoid meeting Calgary in the first round of the playoffs. Paul began rushing with the puck, looking for points, and taking chances. Finally Sather benched him.

—Bob McCammon (1941–), Edmonton Oilers assistant coach, on why Paul Coffey missed breaking Bobby Orr's points record for a defenseman. Coffey missed tying the record by one point, with 138 points to Orr's 139.

Every goal is a highlight film.

> —Ron Francis (1963–), Hartford Whalers center

Nobody ever tells me to give them a pass or anything. My job is to score goals, and if I don't shoot the puck, I can't score goals.

> —Alexander Ovechkin (1985–), Washington Capitals left winger

When I saw that goal, the first thing I said was, "You won't see a goal like that ever again." It's one thing to have second effort but, on top of that, the athleticism he showed. It's just an example of the talent that he has.

> —Sidney Crosby (1987–), Pittsburgh Penguins center, on Alexander Ovechkin's 32nd NHL goal, which he scored while on his back

He's got a tremendous will to score.

> —Paul Kariya (1974–), St. Louis Blues left winger, on Alexander Ovechkin

It felt like a PeeWee game at the end—in all due respect to PeeWees.

> —Glen Hanlon (1957–), Washington Capitals coach, after the Capitals and Calgary Flames scored 6 goals in the last six minutes—and 3 in the final minute—to tie 3–3

The problem is himself.

> —Jacques Lemaire (1945–), Minnesota Wild head coach, on the long scoring slump of Marion Gaborik

I think he knows all my tricks. Or the fact I don't have any tricks.

> —Brendan Shanahan (1969–), New York Rangers left winger, on trying to score against Toronto Maple Leafs goalie Curtis Joseph

Two or three years ago, every game I want to score. And after I score a goal I have a spark, and I'm so happy I want more. Now I'm kind of different. I'm not saying I lost my spark— I still have it—but I don't chase the goal as much as I used to. I'm playing for the team, and I still know I can score, but it's different than two or three years back. Look at great teams like Detroit a couple of years ago; they win the Stanley Cup, and guys only score 25 goals. Nobody has a really big season. You have to play defense, that's how you win.

> –Peter Bondra (1968–), Washington Capitals right winger

I only have one goal in each stick.

> –Petr Klima (1964–), Detroit Red Wings left winger, on his habit of breaking his stick after scoring a goal

I don't mean to sound cocky. But I knew it was just a matter of time before I flipped one in.

> –Ron Hextall (1964–), Philadelphia Flyers goaltender, on becoming the first goaltender to score a goal, December 8, 1987

I need a goal now. I'm looking for the chance all the time. If I get it, and it doesn't jeopardize my team, I'm going for it.

> –Martin Brodeur (1972–), New Jersey Devils goaltender, on scoring a goal. His dreams finally came true during a playoff game against the Montréal Canadiens on April 17, 1997.

I never enjoyed being scored on by anyone, regardless of the situation. During practice it was all business for me. Because of my age, I was constantly working on my angles, and I took a lot of pride in making saves against my teammates or any opponents.

> –Johnny Bower (1924–), Toronto Maple Leafs goaltender

I'm on fire.

> –Darren Langdon (1971–), New Jersey Devils left winger,
> after getting an assist for his first point in 32 games

The biggest thing with a scorer is confidence. When you're younger, you never even think of it, but when you're older, and you stop scoring, you don't walk with the same confidence. You don't have the same arrogance or swagger you once carried onto the ice. You think each scoring chance could be your last, and if you don't score, you're screwed.

> –Pat Verbeek (1964–), New Jersey Devils right winger

Daddy, you're the best hockey player in the world except that you can't score.

> –Clancy Williams, six-year-old daughter of Toronto Maple Leafs
> forward Dave "Tiger" Williams

WINNERS AND LOSERS

In sport winning is everything, but unfortunately there has to be a loser. This is a look into both sides of a game of hockey for the good and for the bad.

It's fun when you're winning.

> —Jacques Plante (1929–86), Montréal Canadiens goaltender

The more pressure there is, the more I like it.

> —Patrick Roy (1965–), Montréal Canadiens goaltender, about his Stanley Cup– and Conn Smythe Trophy–winning performances

I always played best under pressure. Maybe it was the money and the prestige that went with big games.

> —Johnny Bower (1924–), Toronto Maple Leafs goaltender

I thought about buying a lunch bucket and finding a job, but I still wanted to play hockey more than anything. My wife and I decided to sit down and write a letter to every general manager in every league. It cost us all of eight bucks for paper and stamps, and the message was simple—I was out of work and wanted to play. Talk about luck. My letter reached Milt Schmidt of the Bruins just when he was seeking a goalie....I got a call from the Bruins and finally found myself in the NHL. I was 36, one of the oldest rookies ever, and while it was no big deal, I became the first Jewish goaltender in league history.

> —Ross Brooks (1937–), Boston Bruins goaltender, on finally achieving his dream of playing in the NHL

We're very frustrated as a group. It's contagious. Winning's contagious, losing's contagious, and you don't want to get in that mindset.

-Brendan Morrison (1975–), Vancouver Canucks center, after
Vancouver lost 3–0 to Nashville on November 1, 2007, giving
the Canucks a league-worst home record of 1–6–0

I want to win the Stanley Cup. I want to be the best, just the best. I must work. I must learn. Help my team. Hockey is my life, you know. If I do not play hockey, I do not know what I do.

-Alexander Ovechkin (1985–), Washington Capitals left winger

A player must be able to skate, have hockey sense, be able to shoot—not necessarily able to score—and have drive.

-Pierre Pagé (1948–), Québec Nordiques head coach

Put the kids in with a few old pappy guys who still like to win, and the combination is unbeatable.

-Conn Smythe (1895–1980), Toronto Maple Leafs owner and
hockey builder, on the recipe for a winning team

Winning is always fun, but the car is more important.

-Teemu Selänne (1970–), Anaheim Ducks right winger, on the
importance of the All-Star Game. Selänne is an avid car collector.

I'm not sure, I wasn't really paying attention, but I think he was trying to get out of the game.

-Keith Primeau (1971–), Philadelphia Flyers captain, after the
Flyers' goaltender Roman Čechmánek skated to center ice and
started yelling at his team's bench during the fourth game of
the 2002 Eastern Conference quarter finals against the
Ottawa Senators

Let's put it this way: if one of my brothers were standing in
front of the bus last night, and we were about to leave, and
he was on the other team, I'd have run over him. I wouldn't
have called out first to ask him to get out of the way, either.
That's my mentality. That's the way it is. I don't really care.

—Brian Sutter (1956–), St. Louis Blues left winger,
on what it takes to win

Bob [Colorado coach Hartley] asked me after the fourth
goal, when I went to the bench to get some water, "Do you
want to come out?" I said, "No. I'm staying in." I want to
be part of the team. I wanted to be in there in the bumpy
times....I wanted to fight with them as long as I could. But
after the sixth one, that was it.

—Patrick Roy (1965–), Colorado Avalanche goaltender, after
Detroit defeated the Avalanche 7–0 in game seven of the
2002 Western Conference finals

It was designed before to have a Canada-U.S. final, and
you've got that final. They're professional people, those NHL
referees. But they live here [in North America]. They are
Americans and Canadians. They know the players. In crucial
situations, they are going to have human reactions. They're
not going to call a penalty.

—Viacheslav "Slava" Fetisov (1958–), Russian Olympic coach,
after Russia's loss to the United States in the men's
2002 Olympic semifinals

If they'd come out and played the first two periods the way
they played the third, maybe they'd be in this game....But
they didn't play the first 40 minutes. They have nothing to
cry about.

— Kevin Lowe (1959–), Team Canada assistant general manager,
on the same game

When you're losing, Jaromir Jágr is the worst guy in the world to be around because he acts like a suck.

—A former teammate of Jágr's

It's an insult to every parent who has taken their kids to minor hockey at five-thirty in the morning to play hockey. Just like their parents had done for them. You probably had a lot of kids come over from Canada tonight who had a game or practice at seven in the morning and came down to watch tonight. That's an embarrassment to the game and an embarrassment to come out and play like that.

—Andy Murray (1951–), Los Angeles Kings head coach, speaking to his team after a dismal loss in Detroit

I believe fundamentally we are the worst team in the National Hockey League.

—Bobby Holik (1971–), New York Rangers center, after a 9–1 loss to Ottawa

We've got to throw this one out of the window and forget about it.

—Evgeni Nabokov (1975–), San Jose Sharks goaltender, after a tough loss

I simply do not have the words to describe his play! Nobody could expect that 38-year-old Sergei would be able to play so awesome, both in offense and in defense! I think that Fedorov is the great master who helped this team tremendously not only on ice, but also in the locker room because the younger players rubbed off Sergei's work ethic and followed him.

—Victor Tikhonov (1930–), legendary Russian coach, on Sergei Fedorov

You do your job, you get your work done at the rink, and then you go home. The big thing is figuring out what you're going to do the rest of the day.

–Dany Heatley (1981–), Ottawa Senators left winger

Anytime you hold Dallas to a one touchdown, it's not all bad.

–Bobby Smith (1958–), Phoenix Coyotes general manager, after a Coyotes 7–2 loss to the Dallas Stars

It's too easy when you're not winning to look for excuses and point at others for reasons. You can say, "Oh, well, it's this guy's fault or they don't do this well." Or you can say, "I've got to play better and contribute more." You've got to find another gear and come up with big games.

–Sean Burke (1967–), New Jersey Devils goaltender

It hit me like one of Joe Frazier's left hooks. I felt like Dr. Richard Kimble. I felt like, for all these years I've been chasing the one-armed man, and I finally caught him, and it turned out to be the wrong guy.

–Tom McVie (1935–), Boston Bruins assistant coach, on not being hired in 1995 as the next Bruins head coach to replace the outgoing Brian Sutter

I don't like it, and I'm ticked off. If the team wasn't winning or I wasn't doing my job, I would have no problem with this. I've done nothing but work my butt off for this team. They said I wasn't being punished, but it sure does feel like punishment to me. I'm not the type of player who is happy just to be here and collect a paycheck.

–Mike Danton (1980–), New Jersey Devils center, when he was a rookie and was scratched for a game

I was really surprised to win it. I wasn't even thinking about it, really. I'm more happy about winning another Cup, but winning the Conn Smythe is really an honor that I'll never forget.

—Nicklas Lidstrom (1970–), Detroit Red Wings defenseman from Sweden, on being the first European to win the Conn Smythe Trophy

We had absolutely no desire to win. The only desire was to survive, to get to your paycheck. The attitude was terrible, and I made up my mind that if it didn't change I wouldn't be back. I couldn't be associated with it anymore.

—Tony Esposito (1943–), Chicago Blackhawks goaltender, on the bad days in Chicago in the late 1970s

Pride. I get it out of winning.

—Gerry Cheevers (1940–), Boston Bruins goaltender

He epitomizes the term *battler*. You can't define his style. As unorthodox as Dominik Hašek is, and as much of a technician as Patrick Roy is, all you can say about Belfour is that he is a battler. When he won that Cup, that justified saying he is great.

—Peter McNab (1952–), Boston Bruins center, on Dallas Stars goaltender Ed Belfour

We were very close to one another, but I think that winning was the most important thing that we had going for us. When things were not going well, we were frank with one another. Our coaches gave 110 percent, but it was really the players whose pride and deep feelings of commitment sustained the family entity.

—Ralph Backstrom (1937–), Montréal Canadiens center, on the Canadiens in the 1960s

We may not have the greatest hockey club in the world, but it's a club that's loaded with fighting heart. If there's anything that wins hockey championships, it's just that.

–Jack Adams (1895–1968), Detroit Red Wings head coach, on the 1942 Stanley Cup playoffs against the Toronto Maple Leafs

There's nothing wrong with our club physically. It's a question whether or not we've got the stuff that champions are made of. That wasn't hockey out there—it was a fair display of hoodlumism, Detroit's stock in trade! But we've got to adjust ourselves to the Kitty-bar-the-door tactics if we're going to win the Cup.

–Clarence Henry "Hap" Day (1901–90), Toronto Maple Leafs head coach, during their come-from-behind win in the 1942 Stanley Cup finals against the Red Wings

ROOKIES

Everyone has to start somewhere, even the greatest.

My first time out they tried to knock me around quite a bit. Every rookie has to go through this. They knew all the tricks and could make it rough on a kid coming in trying to catch a place on the club. Especially if the kid was only 5'7" and weighed about as much as a sack of potatoes.

–Francis Michael "King" Clancy (1903–86), NHL player, coach and executive, on his first year in the NHL

Bouwmeester has a unique combination of hockey sense, skating ability and stick skills. You know, this is my 29th year in professional hockey, and I've never seen an 18-year-old who's got the complete package like him. He seems to be at the 26- or 27-year-old level, and I'm not talking about average players, I'm talking top players. He's been like that since training camp.

–Paul Baxter (1955–), Florida Panthers assistant coach, on rookie defenseman Jay Bouwmeester

There are three big-league goalies in hockey, and one of them is in the minors.

–Lynn Patrick (1912–80), New York Rangers head coach, after seeing still minor-league goalie Terry Sawchuk's display of goal-tending prowess in his first seven games in the NHL

Phil got both their goals. His little brother making his first NHL start, and he shows me no pity.

–Tony Esposito (1943–), Chicago Blackhawks goaltender, on playing against his brother Phil in his first NHL game

I've never seen a goalie with such fast legs.

> –Jacques Plante (1929–86), Hall of Fame goaltender, on rookie
> goaltender Pelle Lindbergh of the 1980 Philadelphia Flyers

I've worked on my shot a lot. I can hit the net from our zone. I've even practiced a bank shot. I'm just waiting for the right situation.

> –Ron Hextall (1964–), Philadephia Flyers goaltender, on his
> hopes of scoring a goal. He later in fact became the first
> NHL goalie to score.

THE TEAMS

As much as individuals are respected for their skills on the ice, they are nothing without their team. Love them or hate them, hockey is nothing without a team.

Over the last half century, it has been accepted that most fans, as a rule, have two favorite teams—their home team and the Montréal Canadiens. Montréal may not be Paris, but one thinks of it as the Paris of hockey.

–Herbert Warren Wind (1916–2005), American sports journalist

If you work around here long enough, you get a Maple Leaf tattooed on your ass.

–Harold Ballard (1903–90), Toronto Maple Leafs owner,
in a 1980 interview

Every boy in Canada who owns a pair of skates hopes to play for Toronto when he grows up—and most of the good ones do!

–Conn Smythe (1895–1980), Toronto Maple Leafs owner
and hockey builder

Dreams really do come true, I thought to myself as I sat in the stands of Maple Leaf Gardens on that September day in 1973 when I first reported to the Toronto Maple Leafs. The building was dark, and I wanted to be alone, just to have time to think. It was an unbelievable feeling sitting there. I'd finally made it. There I was at the Gardens, about to begin playing for the Maple Leafs, the team I had cheered for like crazy as a kid. I sat there, realizing that everything I had dreamed about had come true.

–Lanny McDonald (1953–), Toronto Maple Leafs forward

The Maple Leafs aren't playing this week, so they aren't losing.

—Dick Beddoes (1926–91), Canadian sports writer

The Forum is hockey's shrine, a glorious melting pot of team, city and sporting tradition—not elegant, not dramatic, not exciting or controversial. It is expansive, yet intimate, exuberant yet unselfconscious. It supports and complements a game, never competing for your attention. And when a game ends, fading away, it gives you nothing to detail the impression it leaves—just a memory of the game and the unshakeable feeling that you've watched it in its proper place.

—Ken Dryden (1947–), Montréal Canadiens goaltender,
from his book *The Game*

When they let me go for a youth movement in 1968, I often joked, "They'll never win another Cup without me." But geez, I didn't mean it!

—Allan Stanley (1926–), Toronto Maple Leafs defenseman

I played and coached against that good Jets team and saw first-hand the way they played the game. I said if I ever was in charge of a team, the Jets style would be the way my team played.

—Glen Sather (1943–), Edmonton Oilers head coach, after seeing
the Winnipeg Jets of the World Hockey Association and their
"firewagon" style of hockey

The box was kind of a gross place to go. The guys in there are bleeding and have bloody noses. They have greenies and yellows and drip all over the boards, and no one's cleaned the place since 1938.

—Dave "Tiger" Williams (1954–), Toronto Maple Leafs forward,
on the penalty box at the old Maple Leaf Gardens in Toronto

I always say to Edmonton people, "It's grand to boast about all the championship teams you've had. But the fact is, you still have to live in Edmonton."

—Russ Peake, Calgary sportscaster

Part of the learning curve in the city of Edmonton is learning to hate the city of Calgary.

—Steve Smith (1963–), Edmonton Oilers defenseman

Our 1951–52 champions that won the playoffs in eight games was the greatest hockey club ever assembled.

—Jack Adams (1895–1968), Detroit Red Wings head coach

Lose a game in this town, and everyone wants to put bullets in the boat. You guys [the media] think this is easy.

—Pat Quinn (1943–), Toronto Maple Leafs head coach

We don't own the team, really. The public of Montréal, in fact the entire province of Québec, owns the Canadiens. The club is more than a professional sports organization, it's an institution, a way of life.

—Senator Hartland Molson (1907–2002),
Montréal Canadiens owner

We were the underdogs so we didn't feel the pressure. Montréal was just going berserk about Expo, and we wanted to do something to deflate a city that assumed the Stanley Cup was going to be part of Expo.

—Frank Mahovlich (1938–), Toronto Maple Leafs left winger, about the 1967 Stanley Cup final between Montréal and Toronto

Montréal will have two teams. One French Canadian and one British Canadian!

–Headline from the *Montréal Gazette* when it was announced that the Montréal Maroons would be joining the NHL in 1924. The Montréal Canadiens were the French team.

People have asked me many times how someone goes about building the kind of tradition the Canadiens have enjoyed for so long. It is really quite simple. You build a top-notch organization manned by the best people at all levels. You get each man doing his job on the ice and off the ice, and all of a sudden you're a winner.

–Sam Pollock (1925–2007), Montréal Canadiens general manager

Those Leafs will know they've had their hides blistered when they get through this series.

–Sid Abel (1918–2000), Detroit Red Wings left winger, speaking prematurely when the Red Wings were up 3–0 on the Toronto Maple Leafs in the 1942 Stanley Cup finals. The Maple Leafs won the Cup 4–3.

Playing the Leafs is like eating Chinese food. Ten minutes later you want to play them again.

–Roger Neilson (1934–2003), journeyman NHL head coach, on his former team

Edmonton with Wayne was a glittering city. Edmonton without Wayne is just another city with a hockey team.

–Dave Lumley (1954–), Edmonton Oilers forward, on former teammate Wayne Gretzky

THE OLD DAYS

Many think of the old days of hockey as a time when gentlemen played the game, but as you will see in many of the following examples, the game was sometimes far from gentle. Hear how hockey actually was back in the early days before most of us were born from people who were there.

Frank and Lester never stopped talking about ways to make the game better. They would throw out new ideas and wanted the other guys to shoot holes in them. The debates often became very heated.

> —Fred "Cyclone" Taylor (1884–1979), Vancouver Millionaires forward, on legendary hockey builders and brothers, Frank and Lester Patrick

Hockey has always been Canada's game. We still play it better that anyone else in the world, and I wish I could lace up my skates right now, and get out there and help keep it that way!

> — Fred "Cyclone" Taylor (1884–1979), Vancouver Millionaires forward, in an interview in 1978

If the players followed my schedule, they'd arrive in Ottawa with plenty of time to get ready. Nothing could be left to chance. We had some good players. Albert Forest, originally from Québec, wasn't even 20 but had great reflexes. J.K. Johnstone worked in the post office. And three of our guys, Norman Watt, George Kennedy and Hector Smith were still digging for gold.

> —Joseph "Klondike Joe" Boyle (1867–1923), entrepreneur and adventurer, on the group of players, the Dawson City Nuggets, he had scrambled together in the Yukon to play the Ottawa Silver Seven in Ottawa for the 1905 Stanley Cup challenge

Hello, Canada, and hockey fans in the United States and Newfoundland!

> —Foster Hewitt (1902–85), Canadian hockey broadcaster, opening the first Hockey Night in Canada radio broadcast in 1931

We lost 9–2, but I was convinced we could catch them next game, especially since we'd have our skating legs. Some of us wondered why they made such a big thing about their supposed star Frank McGee. They say he has only one eye, and I think it showed. We won one battle, however. Watt [Dawson City player] got a stick in the mouth from Moore [Ottawa], so he broke his stick over the Ottawa player's head and knocked him out for 10 minutes.

> —Joseph "Klondike Joe" Boyle (1867–1923), entrepreneur and adventurer, on his Dawson City team's first-game performance

I wasn't very big, but I never backed up an inch. I didn't start much trouble, but if anyone did me dirt, he got it right back.

> —Édouard "Newsy" Lalonde (1887–1970), Montréal Canadiens center

To deport Lalonde to Saskatoon for an unknown player like Joliat is sheer madness. If Joliat can survive two years in the NHL it will be a miracle.

> —Unidentified newspaper columnist, on the 1922 trade that brought Aurel Joliat to the Montréal Canadiens. Joliat lasted 16 seasons with the Canadiens.

Frank and I played our first hockey on the sidewalks of Pointe-St-Charles. We cut sticks from the woods on Nun's Island and used a tin can, a lump of ice, a stone, anything that came handy, for a puck.

> —Lester Patrick (1883–1960), NHL player, coach, general manager, and hockey builder, on his early days in Montréal

I had hooked on to a good job in Québec City which prom-ised a secure future, something hockey in those days couldn't. We mostly played for the love of the game. Guys would get injured, and it ended up that they couldn't work. But we kept coming back. Foolish, some might say, but we loved every second of it.

—Joe Malone (1890–1969), Montréal Canadiens center,
remembering the old days of hockey

Not long ago, taking an aspirin was the medical solution for a concussion.

—Ken Hitchcock (1951–), Columbus Blue Jackets head coach, on
today's increased awareness about this serious hockey health issue

There's no reason why a player is done at 33, 34. They train better, they eat better, they drink better. This isn't the old days when everybody sat around and drank beer.

—Bobby Clarke (1949–), Philadephia Flyers general manager, on
signing Kjell Samuelsson in 1996, when the latter was 38 years old

A few of the rinks were lighted by coal oil lamps, and the corners were dark pockets.

—Fred Waghorne (1866–1956), hockey innovator
and legendary referee

He was even better that they say he was. He'd everything—speed, stickhandling, scoring ability and was a punishing checker. He was strongly built but beautifully proportioned, and he'd an almost animal rhythm.

—Frank Patrick (1885–1958), hockey builder, on Ottawa Silver
Seven center Frank "One-Eyed" McGee

Lalonde was a survivor of a truly permissive age when hockey was genuinely a mug's racket, mottled with roughnecks who preferred to drink an opponent's blood at body temperature, or near there.

–Dick Beddoes (1926–91), Canadian sportswriter,
on Édouard "Newsy" Lalonde

Like his contemporaries Jim Thorpe, Ty Cobb and Jack Johnson, Hobey Baker was a fabulous athlete. Like them he'd a great physique, fantastic reflexes, instant coordination of hand and eye, iron discipline, blazing courage. But to these rare abilities he added another dimension all his own...during his career at Princeton and St. Nick's, he was a college athlete supreme: the gentleman sportsman, the amateur in the pure sense of playing the game *pour le sport*, who never fouled, despised publicity and refused professional offers.

–John Davies, from his book *The Legend of Hobey Baker*

You had to do something. Quite a few of the players could put a curving drop on a shot, and the equipment wasn't exactly the greatest in those days.

–Clint Benedict (1894–1976), Ottawa Senators goaltender

The work of Capt. Reg Noble at center was by far his best effort of the season and bulked big in the St. Pats' success. He showed plenty of hockey north of his shoulder blades. He swung his stick as long as a bass rod, and he broke up play after play in the goulash area in mid-ice.

–Lou Marsh (1879–1936), pioneering Canadian sportswriter

They gave me $600 to use me when and wherever they needed me, and in-between I'd go back and play amateur hockey.

–Harry "Punch" Broadbent (1892–1971), Ottawa Senators right winger, on signing his first contract with the Ottawa in 1912

Nels was the best natural all-round athlete that I have ever seen in Canada and, naturally, over the years that takes in a lot of territory and much consideration, for when he was a kid all the boys of a neighborhood played sports, hard and rough and tumble as was the style of the rather of the rather parochial Hogtown [Toronto] of those times.

–Ted Reeve (1902–83), Canadian sportswriter, on hockey legend Nels Stewart

Paddy Moran was very strong in his work last night, but also very short-tempered. It was due to the referees both being busy watching the play at the Canadiens' end of the rink that he did not get a serious penalty meted out to him when he tried to slash Henri Dallaire's head off with one lightning stroke of his hockey blade.

–Article in the *Montréal Star* after a penalty-filled game between the Québec Bulldogs and the Montréal Canadiens

Bulldogs and the Montréal Canadiens. The most spectacular saves of the match were made by LeSueur. Three of Ottawa's forwards got right down on him when there was no defenseman near enough to help him. First Frank McGee, then Rat Westwick, then Harry Smith shot, but on each occasion, though they were only a yard or two away, he managed to stop the puck and get it to safety. The way he stopped the most dangerous shots was a sight rarely seen.

–Article in the *Montréal Star* on the heroics of goaltending legend Percy LeSueur

In this game Cleghorn made a shambles of the Ottawa team with some assistance from his brother. A vicious swing at Eddie Gerard cut him over the eye for five stitches. Nighbor was charged and in falling damaged his elbow. A butt end for Cy Denneny required several stitches over his eye and more in his nose. This worked out to a match foul and a $15 fine for Sprague. The Ottawa police offered to arrest Sprague and charge him with assault. Lou Marsh, the referee, said he could handle the situation without police interference. Later he wrote in his report that he considered the Cleghorn brothers to be a disgrace to the game of hockey.

–Charles L. Coleman, from his three-volume work, *The Trail of the Stanley Cup*, describing an incident in which the Cleghorn brothers, of the Montréal Canadiens, made their mark on a game against the Ottawa Senators in 1921

If you went to a baseball game and saw Babe Ruth powder one over the fence, you didn't need to know first base from the ass of your pants to realize you had just seen something special. It was the same thing with Morenz. You didn't need to know the difference between a hockey puck and your belly button to know that when you had watched Morenz play the game, you had seen something special.

–Francis Michael "King" Clancy (1903–86), NHL player, coach and executive, on Montréal Canadiens legend Howie Morenz

STANLEY CUP AND THE PLAYOFFS

All their lives they have dreamt of making it far enough in hockey just to get the chance to raise the Stanley Cup high above their heads in triumph. Many have tried, many have failed, but the journey was always fun to watch.

You know, I've held women and babies and jewels and money, but nothing will ever feel as good as holding that Cup.

–Wayne Gretzky (1961–), NHL great

When you win eight straight games in the playoffs, and you win five Cups in a row, there's not a whole lot to get excited about.

–Doug Harvey (1924–89), Montréal Canadiens defenseman, when asked by a reporter if he was excited about winning the Stanley Cup for the fifth time in a row in 1960

Nothing is permanent in this business until you have the Stanley Cup perched on the trophy shelf.

–Tommy Ivan (1911–99), Detroit Red Wings head coach

The playoffs separate the men from the boys, and we found out we have a lot of boys in our dressing room.

–Neil Smith (1955–), New York Rangers general manager, after losing a series to the Washington Capitals

I can't say enough about Boston. I had two cracks at the Cup there. Everyone I played with there has a little piece of this.

–Raymond Bourque (1960–), former Boston Bruins defenseman, after winning his only Stanley Cup with the Colorado Avalanche in 2001

We had no business losing in '67 to Toronto. Terry Sawchuk was the reason. I remember walking in on him all alone in a game in Toronto and how he stopped me. I still can't figure it out. I always had the feeling if I score on that play, if he doesn't make that tremendous save, it very easily could have been another five Stanley Cups in a row.

> –Jean Beliveau (1931–), Montréal Canadiens center on the 1967
> Stanley Cup finals between the Montréal Canadiens and the
> Toronto Maple Leafs

He did the whole load in the Cup. He did everything. That's why our family always laughs when we see players drinking champagne from the Cup.

> –Red Kelly (1927–), Detroit Red Wings defenseman, on the time
> his infant son left behind a few presents in the bowl of the
> Stanley Cup

This dream is gonna last forever. Don't you dare wake me up!

> –Jim Paek (1967–), Pittsburgh Penguins defenseman,
> after winning the Stanley Cup

Excuse me, I'm going to go dive into the Stanley Cup.

> –Mario Lemieux (1965–), Pittsburgh Penguins great, after winning
> his second Stanley Cup against the Blackhawks in 1992

We should've been better, more disciplined. We made untimely mistakes defensively, as a group. This is really humbling for us. After winning the Stanley Cup, we got brought back down to earth, hard. Maybe the humbling is good for us in the long run.

> –Steve Yzerman (1965–), Detroit Red Wings center, following
> Detroit's elimination from the 2007 Stanley Cup playoffs at
> the hands of the Anaheim Ducks

They sat around for 11 days and heard how good they were.
They had a beer here and beer there.

> —John Muckler (1934–), Ottawa Senators general manager, on his
> regrets about not taking his players out of the Canadian capital
> while awaiting their 2007 Stanley Cup final match-up with the
> eventual champion Anaheim Ducks

By the age of 18, the average American has witnessed
200,000 acts of violence on television, most of them occur-
ring during game one of the NHL playoff series.

> —Steve Rushin, American sportswriter

I didn't have any hair anywhere for almost seven months.
So now finally I've got some hair, I'm gonna keep it.

> —Saku Koivu (1974–), Montréal Canadiens captain, who spent most
> of the 2001–02 season undergoing radiation treatment for cancer
> before returning for the playoffs and growing a playoff beard

I hope we can get past Toronto for two reasons. It would be
nice to get to the finals again. But secondly, those guys are so
cocky it's unbelievable.

> —Martin Gélinas (1970–), Carolina Hurricanes left winger,
> during the 2002 Eastern Conference final between the
> Hurricanes and the Maple Leafs

Better's a tough word. You win by one goal in seven games.
They played unbelievable. It could have gone either way.
Basically, it was just the last man standing. We might have
won one more battle or got one more big save. There are so
many little things you can break it down to. Two teams sepa-
rated by one goal in seven games.

> —Brad Richards (1980–), Tampa Bay Lightning center, when
> asked what made Tampa Bay the better team in the
> 2005 Stanley Cup final

I can't hear what Jeremy says, because I've got my two
Stanley Cup rings plugging my ears.

> –Patrick Roy (1965–), Colorado Avalanche goaltender, responding
> to the criticisms of Chicago Blackhawks center Jeremy Roenick
> during the 1996 playoff series

I don't even recognize myself anymore. I'm saving up for
a Zamboni. I'm looking for a summer home in Medicine
Hat. I'm shaving with a Lady Byng. I wanna torch my stick.
I wanna kiss the post. And to think I used to think a Stanley
Cup had something to do with an athletic supporter and a drill.
I admit, I'm still learning. For instance, I'm having a little
trouble seeing the blue dot on the puck when I'm actually at
the games, but I'm picking it up on TV pretty easy, that's for
sure. And best of all; no Li'l Penny!

> –Rick Reilly (1958–), American sportswriter, writing in
> *Sports Illustrated* on the hockey fever in his native Colorado
> during the Avalanche's first season in Denver

The remedy, right now, is two scotches and an aspirin, I think.

> – Harry Sinden (1932–), Boston Bruins general manager, after his
> team was eliminated from the playoffs

We're scared of losing. That's why we win. We know what it's
like to lose, and we hate it. We enjoy being champions too
much.

> –Bob Bourne (1954–), New York Islanders left winger,
> on the Islanders dynasty in the early 1980s

When your team finished first and goes on to win the Stanley
Cup in your rookie season, that's quite a thrill.

> –Cecil R. "Tiny" Thompson (1905–81), Boston Bruins goaltender,
> when the Bruins won the 1929 Stanley Cup

When we were shaking hands with the other team, I basically left it up to him. If he was willing to shake my hand, I was willing to shake his. I was willing to put it behind me. I wasn't proud of what happened, and I left it up to him to shake my hand. He did, so that's the end of it, hopefully.

–Scott Niedermayer (1973–), New Jersey Devils defenseman, on getting past a blow to the head he delivered to Florida Panthers tough guy Peter Worell on March 19, 2000

Well, last night they did a bit, definitely. We still have two more wins to get in this playoff series. If we don't do that, last night was worth nothing, so you can't let that happen until you've won the series.

–Scott Niedermayer (1973–), New Jersey Devils defenseman, when asked if the Toronto Maple Leafs looked a little shaken by their performance in the 2000 Eastern Conference semifinals

We're definitely a really good team, up with the top teams in the NHL. Obviously, the 1995 team, when you win the Stanley Cup, there's no team better than you, and we still have a ways to go to get there. Similarities would be, obviously with Marty Brodeur in net, that's one. There were a few guys back here in '95 who know what it takes to go all the way. We also have some new guys who are excited to be here and excited to be in the playoffs, so I think it's a good mix.

–Scott Niedermayer (1973–), New Jersey Devils defenseman, on the Devils' run to the Stanley Cup in 2000

You look at what Nicklas Lidstrom did all the way through the playoffs, and he was just about a perfect player on the ice. It's really a wonderful tribute to him.

–William Scott "Scotty" Bowman (1933–), Detroit Red Wings head coach, after the Red Wings won the 2002 Stanley Cup. Bowman announced his retirement at the end of the last game.

We know the exhilarating feeling only a player on a Stanley Cup winner can appreciate.

> –Bernard Marcel "Bernie" Parent (1945–), Philadelphia Flyers goaltender, after winning his second Cup with the Flyers in 1975

When it came to the playoffs, I always seemed to get on a roll. There was more pressure, which helped my concentration, and the game seemed a little easier.

> –Billy Smith (1950–), New York Islanders goaltender

Nothing has ever matched that thrill!

> –Lorne "Gump" Worsley (1929–2007), Montréal Canadiens goaltender, after tasting champagne from his first Stanley Cup, in 1965

When we won against Philly, we had to create an example. You don't have to be big and rough and fight all the time to win the Stanley Cup. We had the size, and we had the scorers. If you don't score, you don't win, no matter how good a fighter you are.

> –Yvon Cournoyer (1943–), Montréal Canadiens forward, on beating the famed "Broad Street Bullies," as the Philadelphia Flyers were called, in the 1976 Stanley Cup

I remember sitting in that dressing room, waiting for the fourth game to start. The only thing on our minds was, we can't go back to Toronto if we lose this game too. We were thinking we couldn't lose four straight and face the people back home.

> –Syl Apps (1915–98), Toronto Maple Leafs center, on the 1942 Stanley Cup final against the Detroit Red Wings. Toronto won the next four games to take the Cup.

Tasted like horse pee from a tin cup.

—Lorne "Gump" Worsley (1929–2007), Montréal Canadiens goaltender, on drinking champagne from the Stanley Cup, presumably when the thrill had worn off slightly

If we do win this thing, that Cup's going to be beside me at the altar. I hope the wife doesn't get too mad.

—Olaf Kölzig (1970–), Washington Capitals goaltender, on his upcoming wedding after the 1998 Stanley Cup finals. She was fine: the Caps lost to the Red Wings in four straight games.

PERSONALITIES

Hockey is full of colorful characters whose influence, both good and bad, has continually molded the character of the game as we know it.

Don is widely known as Grapes. If his last name were Grapes, he'd likely be known as Cherry.

> –Trent Frayne (1918–), Canadian sportswriter, on hockey commentator Don Cherry

I don't think anybody in this country speaks for the right-wing guy, the guy that gets up at six in the morning and works from seven to five and pays the freight.

> –Don Cherry (1934–), Canadian hockey commentator

I led the league in hangovers. Fourteen years, every day.

> –Gary Smith (1944–), NHL goaltender, who played on eight different teams in his 14-year career

I do think the media blew up the fact that I was throwing up. When I threw up, I felt like I was doing what I needed to do to prepare for the game. I felt that if I threw up, I played better.

> –Glenn Hall (1931–), Chicago Blackhawks goaltender, on his strange habit of throwing up before a game and even between periods

I don't mind Pavel Bure or Alexei Yashin. I don't mind Markus Naslund. But if you get Europeans who don't score, they're useless, because they don't do anything else.

> –Don Cherry (1934–), Canadian hockey commentator

Yeah, I'm cocky, and I am arrogant. But that doesn't mean I'm not a nice person.

—Jeremy Roenick (1970–), San Jose Sharks forward

He liked to present himself as this moody, aloof person, because then people would leave him alone. One time a young boy got hit with a puck during a game. They brought him into the dressing room afterward, and Terry got his stick signed by all the players and gave it to the boy. Then he turned to me and said, "If you tell the press about this, I'll kill you." That's the way he was.

—Marcel Pronovost (1930–), Detroit Red Wings defenseman, on his teammate Terry Sawchuk

Harold Ballard promised me complete control, but I felt that he would not keep his nose out of the operation, that he would want to be the guy quoted in the press about the team. I just couldn't see working under those conditions.

—William Scott "Scotty" Bowman (1933–), Detroit Red Wings head coach, on the prospect of working for Toronto Maple Leafs owner Harold Ballard

Baby Blue was a gamer, but she was like a good rookie defenseman trying to replace Bobby Orr. We had a good time with Baby, but there really could only be one Blue.

—Don Cherry (1934–), Canadian hockey commentator, on his dogs Blue and Baby Blue

I start thinking about what I'm going to wear the next morning. I get the suit or jacket that I'm going to wear, and I hang it up in my bedroom. Before I go to bed, I put different ties with it. So I'm thinking about that suit all week.

—Don Cherry (1934–), Canadian hockey commentator, on picking out his wardrobe for his *Coach's Corner* segment on CBC's *Hockey Night in Canada*

Chris is a good, solid guy. He does have that switch where he can snap, and I think that's why he's been in the league for so long.

> —Bryan Berard (1977–), New York Islanders defenseman, on former Islanders teammate Chris Simon. Simon now plays in Russia.

As always, I remain hopeful that Don Cherry won't be offered the same-length contract.

> —Ron MacLean (1960–), Canadian hockey commentator and Don Cherry straight man, on his recent four-year contract renewal

My weapon isn't my shot. It's me.

> —Alexander Ovechkin (1985–), Washington Capitals left winger

Biologically, I'm 10. Chronologically, I'm 33. In hockey years, I'm 66.

> —Mark Messier (1961–), NHL great

I guess they respect my shot because they were all ready at the blue line.

> —Patrick Roy (1965–), Colorado Avalanche goaltender, on his attempt at the Edmonton Oilers empty net

So many people in television don't say what they think. They're a bit phony. But [Cherry] touches a nerve in this country. He says what a lot of people are afraid to say. I've worked with him for 20 years, and he's the same off the air as he is on the air. This is not an act, and people respect sincerity.

> —Brian Williams (1946–), Canadian sportscaster, on hockey commentator Don Cherry

Jack Darragh was one of the most temperamental players that ever figured in the National Hockey League. Jack had a strange disposition and at times it was almost impossible to humor him. In fact, it was just through luck and good judgment that we attracted him back to Toronto for the final game of the memorable series of 1920. Following Ottawa's defeat in the first match at Toronto, Darragh threw down his skates and announced that he was going home to Ottawa. He dashed out of the arena, jumped into a taxi and made his train connections before we could persuade him to return. "I've had enough hockey for this winter," Darragh shouted. "You will have to get along without me in the final game." Some of the club owners and players were in favor of letting Darragh remain in Ottawa, but we thought the matter over and finally sent him a rush message as follows: "Nighbor and Gerard have taken sick. Don't throw us down. We need you for the game tomorrow, and the world championship is at stake." So the midnight express out of Ottawa brought Darragh up to Toronto again.

–Tommy Gorman (1886–1961), founding member of the
National Hockey League and longtime NHL head coach
and general manager

I consider my style that of the men of the 1930s, where men had an elegant style, tight suits, tight collars, lots of jewelry, a clean sharp image. I must admit my style has been called foppish, but I like it.

–Don Cherry (1934–), Canadian hockey commentator

Jerk that he is, he's always wearing that smirking grin that makes you want to punch him in the face.

–Mike Milbury (1952–), New York Islanders general manager,
on defenseman Ulf Samuelsson

When he was with us in the dressing room and off the ice, he was an easygoing guy. But we had this anteroom off of the dressing room, and during games, the only one allowed in there between periods was Bill. He'd be in there, smoking a cigarette. That was where he found his solace from the game, his solitude.

–Ken Reardon (1921–2008), Montréal Canadiens defenseman, on Canadiens teammate, goaltender Bill Durnan

A goaltender has to protect his crease. If they're going to come that close, I have to use any means to get them out of there. If I have to use my stick, I'll use my stick.

–Billy Smith (1950–), New York Islanders goaltender

He realized that the only team that could beat our team was ourselves. We had such a good team that petty little grievances could develop that might bring the team down. So what Scotty did, he made himself the focal point. The one thing we had in common was that everybody hated Scotty.

–Steve Shutt (1952–), Montréal Canadiens forward, on the mood in the Canadiens locker room during their 1970s dynasty under coach Scotty Bowman

They can't keep me out of Maple Leaf Gardens. I'll buy my way into the place!

–Jack Adams (1895–1968), Detroit Red Wings head coach, on being thrown out of Maple Leaf Gardens after getting into a fight with a referee during a game

INTERNATIONAL FLAVOR

Hockey has become a truly international sport, and some truly great games have been played on the international level, in the Olympics, World Cup and IIHL World Championships. But many still believe that the greatest international hockey ever was the 1972 Summit Series between Canada and the Soviet Union.

One thing we really learned from them is interference. Until 1972, interference in the NHL was something the refs called closely, and there was very little of it. The Soviets were masters of it in 1972, and it got under our players' skins when it wasn't called. Fred Shero [coach of the 1970s Philadelphia Flyers] was a big devotee of the Soviet style, and he had the Flyers setting picks a great deal. Since then, interference, which many call obstruction, has been the NHL's biggest problem because not enough of it gets called.

–Harry Sinden (1932–), Boston Bruins general manager

At that point, there was an absolutely sickening feeling. We all knew that the sleeping giant had been awoken, and we were going to have a fight on our hands.

–Paul Henderson, (1943–), Toronto Maple Leafs left winger, on losing the first game of the 1972 Summit Series to the Soviets as a member of Team Canada

So what if we didn't score? I was thinking of switching to journalism anyway.

–Vladimir Yurzinov (1940–), HC Dynamo Moscow star in the 1960s

The Russians have always been superbly conditioned athletes, good skaters with fundamental skills, discipline in their play, stamina to sustain a fast pace for 60 minutes and an excellent transition game, going from defense to offense very quickly. Funny isn't it, but that's the description of many Stanley Cup winners.

–Harry Sinden, (1932–), Boston Bruins general manager, on the 1972 Soviet team

We don't care about Canada. We don't take them as the team to beat. I don't think they're even close to being the best team in the tournament. You've seen the by the scores.

–Martin Ručinsky (1971–), St. Louis Blues forward, playing for the Czech Republic during the 2002 Olympic Winter Games, on eventual gold-medal winner Team Canada

Most people have friends, but no money. I have the opposite. I don't have a chance to talk to my real friends, the ones I've had since I was five years old. Sometimes I wish I could bring Czechoslovakia to America. Then I would be the happiest guy in the world.

–Jaromir Jágr (1972–), New York Rangers forward

I used to bring a crock pot on the bus in junior and cook Kraft Dinner. I just ate a lot of noodles. It's that simple.

–Jamie McLennan (1971–), former NHL goalie now playing in Japan, on the origin of his nickname, "Noodles"

Vokie's wife, Stumpy's wife, my girlfriend, and sometimes Stumpy's grandma—I eat everything from them. It's good because you can spend time with them, watch Czech movies, do lots of things.

–Rostislav Olesz (1985–), Florida Panthers forward from the Czech Republic, on his appreciation for Czech women such as his girlfriend, Tomas Vokoun's wife and Josef Stumpel's wife and grandmother

Not even in Canada have I seen anything like this. And their coach is going to be the next national team coach. If this is the future of ice hockey, I advise everyone to stop playing.

—Alpo Suhonen (1948–), Helsingin IFK and former Chicago Blackhawks head coach, after a SM-liiga (Finnish league) game against rival Jokerit, which Suhonen called the dirtiest game he's ever coached

It wasn't pretty what I said. Basically, I told him, "I've been in this league a long time and I have about two years left, so I've got nothing to lose. You've got your whole career ahead of you. You try that sh** with me again and I'll f***ing take you out for good. Your career ends. You think I'm kidding?"

—Petr Svoboda (1966–), former NHL defenseman and member of the Czech national team, recalling a conversation with Russian right winger and fellow NHLer Pavel Bure during the 1998 Olympic gold-medal game. In a previous game, Bure had hit Svoboda in the face with the butt end of his stick, just missing Svoboda's eye and leaving a long abrasion on his cheek.

This is definitely the best team I have played [on] in the National Hockey League, but in Russia, the teams I played for were some of the best teams in the history of the game.

—Igor Larionov (1960–), Detroit Red Wings center from Russia, on the 2002 Stanley Cup–winning Red Wings

It now turns out that the French woman judge Marie-Reine Le Gougne should have been a hockey official, because both Canada's artistic presentation and their technical merit marks here at hockey would be very low.

—Jim Lampley (1949–), American sportscaster, after Canada opened the 2002 Winter Olympics men's hockey tournament with a loss to Sweden and a slim victory over Germany

The mood is like we killed somebody or stole something.

–Ján Filc (1953–), Slovakian national coach, after the team failed to
advance from the preliminary round at the 2002 Winter Olympics

They Shamed Their Country.

–Front page headline in a Swedish newspaper, the day after Belarus
upset the Swedes in the men's quarterfinals in the 2002 Winter
Olympics. The article included photos of every Swedish player,
identified by name and NHL salary.

Practice is cancelled tomorrow. No one else left to beat.

–Sign posted in the Team Canada dressing room after their 3–2
victory over Finland in the 2004 World Cup final

All my friends, tons of my friends….Everybody, my family, my
close friends, supported me….I simply don't know what to say.
This victory is for all Russian people, for our country. Guys, we
are with you, this victory is for you! Finally we won the gold
you were dreaming of, you were talking of, and we deserved it.
We all love you. Let's go, Russia! We are the Champions!

–Alexander Ovechkin (1985–), Washington Capitals left winger
and Russian team member, on Russia's winning the 2008 IIHF
World Championships

I had accomplished everything I could in hockey at home. I
asked to be allowed to move to North America to play, but
I was turned down. I wanted to test myself in pro hockey
and was able to find a way out of the country.

–Václav Nedomansky (1944–), Detroit Red Wings center,
on wanting to leave his native Czechoslovakia

If I had stayed in Slovakia, I probably wouldn't be playing
hockey today, I'm sure. It was probably the best thing that
happened to me.

–Zdeno Chára (1977–), Boston Bruins defenseman

Everybody knows [Ilya Kovalchuk] is a great player, and he's got a great shot. He started to score at the right time. He won the game, and it's great for us. You know what? I think the whole team believed from the start to finish that we could win this game. We have a great team and great players. We believe in each other. [As for Evgeni Nabokov], he's our best player. He's the best goalie in the world. He did a great job for us. He was just unbelievable. It's special for defensemen to play in front of him. You know, it's not about whether you're tired. It's about what's in your heart.

—Andrei Markov (1978–), Montréal Canadiens defenseman and
Russian team member, after Russia won the 2008 IIHF gold medal

This is great! We've been waiting for this for 15 years. It's always great to win, but it's a team effort, and we have a great group of guys here. The players, the coaches...everybody has been positive all the time. We felt a good pressure. We knew that I don't know how many million people would be watching us. [For my winning goal], we have a power play, and Fedorov, he's 38 years old, but he's brought so much patience and intensity to the team, and he makes that great pass to me. Then, I was one-on-one with the goalie, and I just shot it in. The [team's] leaders trust us and we trust them. Now we'll have a huge party—it's vacation time now. We have a chartered plane to Russia tomorrow, and we'll have a party there.

—Ilya Kovalchuk (1983–), Atlanta Thrashers left winger and
Russian team member, after scoring the winning goal in the
gold-medal game against Canada at the 2008 IIHF
World Championships

The Summit Series not only produced some of the finest hockey the world had seen, it also encouraged a look at how the game is played across the globe. The series and the fact that the Russians were a superb team opened up healthy discussions on the state of hockey.

—Harry Sinden (1932–), Boston Bruins general manager

LOST IN TRANSLATION

Hockey began with a language issue, and tensions between French Canadian players and their Anglo counterparts fueled many early rivalries. Now, over a quarter of the players in the NHL are European, and the mix of language and background presents an even greater challenge in the race to produce winning teams.

American professional athletes are bilingual; they speak English and profanity.

–Gordie Howe (1928–), Detroit Red Wings great

They do a lot of talking, but I'm not sure they actually understand each other.

–Darren McCarty (1972–), Detroit Red Wings forward, on teammates Vladimir Konstantinov and rival Claude Lemieux

At the end of the movie, there was a standing ovation in the theatre. I just left. To be honest, I felt like I'd lost. My friends played there—Krutov, Makarov, Fetisov, Kasatonov. I wish the guys in Hollywood had spent more time, maybe even just five minutes, to show the Russian side of the story. They should have showed a little bit of what happened inside the Soviet camp. But I know American movies are always like that.

–Igor Larionov (1960–), Detroit Red Wings center, who was too young to play for the Soviets at the 1980 Olympics, on the movie *Miracle*, about the 1980 gold-medal-winning U.S. men's hockey team

Hell, I don't know if he speaks French.

–Hector "Toe" Blake (1912–95), Montréal Canadiens head coach, when asked if the quiet rookie Henri Richard spoke English

He brings something special. I don't know what it is, but if you ask him, you couldn't understand his answer.

> –Wayne Gretzky (1961–), NHL great, on Edmonton Oilers teammate Esa Tikkanen

I no believe in pyramids. I no believe in any man upstairs. I just believe in the big fellow.

> –Borje Salming (1951–), Toronto Maple Leafs defenseman from Sweden, with his limited English, referring to himself

They ask me, "Is this really your name?" Only in America.

> –Miroslav Šatan (1974–), New York Islanders forward from the Czech Republic, on the frequent questions he receives regarding his last name

Being called a frog 20 times a day is something that ends up getting on your nerves.

> –Martin Lapointe (1973–), Ottawa Senators forward, on a fight he had with his Team Canada teammate Eric Lindros before the 1991 Junior World Championships

Every time a puck gets past me, and I look back in my net, I say "Oh, oh."

> –Bernard Marcel "Bernie" Parent (1945–), former Philadelphia Flyers goaltender, on why he chose to wear the number 00 in the World Hockey Association

Luc Robitaille is a great kid and a good player, but ask anybody on the street, and they'd probably think Luc Robitaille is a type of salad dressing.

> –Bruce McNall (1950–), Los Angeles Kings owner

He's one of those guys whose English gets worse every year. But as long as it doesn't affect his play, we're all right.

> –Wade Belak (1976–), Toronto Maple Leafs forward, on teammate Tomáš Kaberle

SUPERSTITIONS

*Good luck charms and pre-game rituals have always been
a part of the tricks NHL players have used to get them
into the "zone" to win.*

I just don't like anyone touching my sticks.

—Steve Shutt (1952–), Montréal Canadiens forward, on his habit of
carefully preparing his sticks before a game

I usually don't let anyone touch my stick before the game.

—Sidney Crosby (1987–), Pittsburgh Penguins center

I don't like my hockey sticks touching other sticks, and I don't
like them crossing one another, and I kind of have them hid-
den in the corner. I put baby powder on the ends. I think it's
essentially a matter of taking care of what takes care of you.

—Wayne Gretzky (1961–), NHL great

Fire me, Major, and you'll never finish first. I'll put a curse
on this team that will hoodoo it until the end of time.

—Pete Muldoon (1881–1929), first Chicago Blackhawks head
coach. The "Curse of Muldoon" is actually fictional. It was attrib-
uted to Muldoon when he was fired by team owner Frederic
McLaughlin after losing to the Boston Bruins in the 1927 playoffs
but was actually written by Toronto *Globe and Mail* writer Jim
Coleman in 1943. The curse seemed real because the Blackhawks
did not finish in first place from 1927 until the 1966–67 season.

Before every game, I make a cross out of adhesive tape and
stick it to my locker in the dressing room.

—Félix Potvin (1971–), Toronto Maple Leafs goaltender

I always put my equipment on the same way: left shin pad, left stocking, right shin pad, right stocking. Then pants, left skate, right skate, shoulder pads, elbow pads—first the left, then the right—and finally, the jersey, with the right side tucked into my pants.

—Wayne Gretzky (1961–), NHL great

I never get my hair cut when we're on the road because the last time I did, we lost.

—Wayne Gretzky (1961–), NHL great

During the warm-up, I always shoot my first puck way off to the right of the goal. I go back to the dressing room and drink a Diet Coke, a glass of iced water, a Gatorade and another Diet Coke.

—Wayne Gretzky (1961–), NHL great

I am always the last player on the team to put on my uniform before a game.

—Chris Chelios (1962–), Detroit Red wings defenseman

Before every game, I meticulously lay out each piece of my equipment on the locker room floor, and I always dress myself in the same order.

— Patrick Roy (1965–), Montréal Canadiens goaltender,
on his pre-game routine

On the day of a game, I never speak to anybody after one-thirty in the afternoon.

—Stéphane Quintal (1986–), Montréal Canadiens defenseman

In between periods, I put my stick away myself, always in the same place.

> —Petr Svoboda (1966–), Tampa Bay Lightning defenseman

In between periods, I always ask for a drink made with 50 percent Coke and 50 percent water. I've had this habit ever since I started to play for the Canadiens.

> —Bob Gainey (1953–), Montréal Canadiens forward,
> now the Canadiens' general manager

I hit the posts and the crossbar at the beginning of every period and during the intermissions.

> —Ron Hextall (1964–), Philadephia Flyers goaltender,
> on his habit of smacking the posts

On the day of a game, I get up at 8:30 AM. I have my usual breakfast, orange juice, oatmeal, two slices of bread, and a glass of milk. Then I head off to team training. When I get back, I always eat a hamburger steak and watch a show on TV. I have a 90-minute nap in the afternoon. Four hours before the game, I eat a plate of spaghetti. I arrive at the locker room at around 5:00 PM, and I put on my underwear. In the two and a half hours before warm-up, I chew 20 to 25 sticks of gum and drink lots of water. I tape up my three or four sticks for the game, and, before every game, I jump in the dressing room spa for three or four minutes. Then I put on the rest of my equipment.

> —Stéphane Lebeau (1968–), Montréal Canadiens center

I hate the color black, so I always use white tape on my stick.

> —Guy Carbonneau (1960–), Montréal Canadiens center,
> now the Canadiens' head coach

NOT SO SMART

Most players in the NHL can be brilliant on the ice.
Off the ice is another story.

Bob Kelly was so dumb, they should have written his name on the Stanley Cup in crayon.

> —Gene Hart (1931–99), Philadelphia Flyers announcer.

That's so when I forget how to spell my name, I can still find my [expletive] clothes.

> —Stu Grimson (1965–), Chicago Blackhawks left winger, explaining why he kept a color photo of himself above his locker

S-C-O-R-E!

> —Eddie Shack (1937–), Toronto Maple Leafs right winger, after scoring a goal, to the interviewer who had told him, "You can't spell *goal*, much less score one."

What sport does *Hockey Night in Canada* cover?

> —Terry Johnson, humorist

You can always get someone to do your thinking for you.

> —Gordie Howe (1928–), Detroit Red Wings great, after being asked why hockey players always wear a protective cup and rarely a helmet

They always try to play with our minds. But that won't work with our club. We've got 20 guys without brains.

> —Bobby Clarke (1949–), Philadephia Flyers general manager

It's about 40 percent technique and about 75 percent strength.

> —Patrice Brisebois (1971–), Montréal Canadiens defenseman,
> on why he lost a fight to the much smaller Theoren Fleury

There's a thousand theories, but theories are for scientists. We're too stupid for that. We've just got to get back to the Xs and Os.

> —Mike Ricci (1971–), San Jose Sharks center, on San Jose's slow
> start in the 2002–03 season

Robbie told me not to think anymore. Thinking doesn't really accomplish anything; it just gets in the way. He wanted to say he's got no rhyme or reason to what he does, but deep down he does.

> —Steve Shields (1972–), Boston Bruins goaltender, explaining the
> latest advice from his coach, Robbie Ftorek

We're not sharp on the bench. I know I get screwed up sometimes going left to right, but if you can count to five that's the main thing. We've got a few who have a problem.

> —Markus Naslund (1973–), Vancouver Canuck left winger, on the
> team's number of bench minors for too many men on the ice

I'd say there's 100 percent of the guys who think they're in the 25 percent.

> —Doug Weight (1971–), St. Louis Blues left winger, on teammate
> Brett Hull's claim that 75 percent of the players in the NHL
> were overpaid

Fifty percent of the game is mental, and the other 50 percent is being mental. I've got that part down no problem.

> —Basil McRae (1961–), Minnesota North Stars left winger

I am 10 times smarter than everyone else in this game—
beyond a shadow of a doubt.

–Brett Hull (1964–), St. Louis Blues right winger

I've never had major knee surgery on any other part of my body.

–Saku Koivu (1974–), Montréal Canadiens captain

I can't say that my way to the NHL was littered with
blueberries.

–Krzysztof Oliwa (1973–), New Jersey Devils left winger
from Poland

We have only one person to blame, and that's each other.

–Barry Beck (1957–), New York Rangers defenseman,
after a tough loss

It was 1998, and I made mistakes. It wasn't smart; it was stupid.

–Jaromir Jágr (1972–), New York Rangers forward, on losing
$500,000 on a gambling website

I was never going to be a player to get standing ovations in
a visitor's building. I realized that from day one, the way I
played, I'd never be a Gretzky or a Lemieux. Well, a Mario,
I mean.

–Claude Lemieux (1965–), Dallas Stars right winger,
forgetting himself for a second

One road trip we were stuck on the runway for seven hours.
The plane kept driving and driving until we arrived at the
rink, and then I realized we were on a bus.

–Glenn Healy (1962–), Toronto Maple Leafs goaltender,
on his time in the minor leagues

When I came to the Rangers, I wanted to be a defenseman, but nobody would chip in for an operation to have half my brain removed.

—Bob Froese (1958–), New York Rangers goaltender

It takes brains. It's not like a forward, where you can get away with scoring and not play defense. On defense you have to be thinking.

—Chris Chelios (1962–), Detroit Red Wings defenseman

I've got nothing to say, and I'm only gonna say it once!

—Floyd Smith (1935–), Toronto Maple Leafs head coach, after a bad loss

At the end of the day, the sun's going to come up.

—Jean-Sébastien Giguère (1977–), Anaheim Ducks goaltender, on staying positive after a 5–1 loss to the Edmonton Oilers

I couldn't believe they'd beaten me on the play. I was sure the puck didn't quite cross the goal line. So I looked up at the big screen to watch the replay. Perhaps it would confirm I was right. While I was watching the replay, the referee dropped the puck and the play resumed. The Washington centerman won the draw and slipped the puck over to hard-shooting Mike Gartner. He stepped over the blue line and rifled a shot in my direction. But I didn't see the puck coming because I was still watching the replay on the giant screen. That's when I heard my teammates screaming at me to wake up, and suddenly I knew I'd made a terrible faux pas.

—John Garrett (1951–), Vancouver Canucks goaltender, on letting in his worst goal ever

We can't have stupidity in our locker room, and we can't have stupidity on the ice. The stupidity has all been used up, plus some, in the NHL this year. The stupidity meter is broken.

> –Jeremy Roenick (1970–), Philadelphia Flyers center

I was young and stupid then. Now, I'm not young anymore.

> –Jyrki Lumme 1966–), Toronto Maple Leafs defenseman,
> on his early years playing for Montréal

TOUGH GUYS

Enforcers are part of the way the North American game is played. You don't like it? Get out of the way!

We take the shortest route to the puck and arrive in ill humor.

–Bobby Clarke, (1949–), Philadephia Flyers center, on the rough and tough persona of the 1970s Flyers, known as "the Broad Street Bullies"

Most people who don't know I play hockey think I was thrown through a plate-glass window or something.

–Theoren Fleury (1968–), Calgary Flames right winger, on the many bumps and bruises he received in his career

The guys tell me I have nothing to protect—no brain, no pain.

–Randy Carlyle (1956–), Winnipeg Jets defenseman, on not wearing a helmet

There's a difference between a hockey player and a football player or a baseball player. It's that hockey guys play if they can breathe.

–Conn Smythe (1895–1980), Toronto Maple Leafs owner and hockey builder

For the most part, with the possible exception of me, I don't think anybody goes out to try to hurt somebody.

–Jeremy Roenick (1970–), San Jose Sharks center

Dirty isn't a derogatory word—it's a good thing to be in hockey.

–Steve Yzerman (1965–), Detroit Red Wings center, when asked about former Washington Capitals center Dale Hunter's playing style

You got to hit first.

> –Brian "Spinner" Spencer (1949–88), Toronto Maple Leafs
> left winger

I don't even like talking about fighting. It's not an honor. As a kid, I was always the top scorer on my team. Would I rather have a good fight or a goal? I celebrate every goal like it's my last.

> –Georges Laraque (1976–), Edmonton Oilers right winger, after
> being voted as the NHL's top fighter by *The Hockey News* in 2003

Intimidation's always going to be part of our game. I just don't know about standing back and watching two guys fight two or three times in a game.

> –Wayne Gretzky (1961–), NHL great

I'd rather fight than score.

> –Dave "The Hammer" Schultz (1949–), Philadelphia Flyers
> right winger

If hockey fights were fixed, I'd be in more of them.

> –Rod Gilbert (1941–), New York Rangers right winger

All other players had to test us. We were just chicken hockey players from Europe. For a couple of years, it was "chicken Swede" this and "chicken Swede" that. I never hear it anymore. A few elbows took care of that.

> –Borje Salming, (1951–), Toronto Maple Leafs defenseman

If I play badly, I'll pick a fight in the third, just to get into a fight. I'll break a guy's leg to win, I don't care. Afterward I say, "Yeah, all right, I played badly, but I won the fight so who gives a damn."

> –Derek Sanderson (1946–), Boston Bruins center

All my friends back home fight on the street, and all they get
is arrested.

> —Patrick Cote (1975–), Nashville Predators enforcer,
> on his $375,000 salary

Wayne came over to the bench one day after seeing Chára
and said, "That's why I'm quitting."

> —John Muckler (1934–), New York Rangers coach, on the
> soon-to-retire Wayne Gretzky's reaction to 6'9" New York
> Islanders defenseman Zdeno Chára

The bigger they are, the harder they hit.

> —Mike O'Connell (1955–), Boston Bruins assistant general man-
> ager, on acquiring 6'4" left winger Ken Belanger in 1998

As they mature as players and get used to the pro lifestyle,
they kind of want to look like their bankbook. They want to
be a little more dignified, but there's no job for them in that
arena. They forget what got them there, and they're not
around very long.

> —Dave "Tiger" Williams (1954–), Los Angeles Kings forward,
> on the modern NHL tough guy

Does anybody want that job? Anybody who says yes, you
know the guy's an idiot. You just do what you do. And then
again, you get in that lane, and you better stay in that lane,
or you won't be in any lane.

> —Dave "Tiger" Williams (1954–), Los Angeles Kings forward,
> on the enforcers

I've always felt we weren't physical enough on the back line.
Now there's a no-parking sign in front of our net.

> —Dean Lombardi (1958–), San Jose Sharks general manager,
> on acquiring enforcer Marty McSorley

We got suspensions for laying people low, not head shots. Bullies? People forget, every night was a 20-minute brawl and three-and-a-half-hour game because of the fights. Under today's rules, every hit from our era would be a two-minute or five-minute penalty.

–Bob "Hound Dog" Kelly (1950–), former Philadelphia Flyers left winger, on the difference between the 1970s "Broad Street Bullies" and the roster that accumulated five suspensions for dirty hits during the early part of the 2007–08 season

Dion doesn't know any name plates, he just knows sweater colors. And that's the great thing about his game.

–Mike Keenan (1949–), Calgary Flames head coach, on the physical approach defenseman Dion Phaneuf takes with opposing forwards

Men will be men. You mark your territory, and I'm going to mark mine.

–Tony Twist (1968–), St. Louis Blues left winger, on why fighting will always be part of hockey

Just charge me with the usual.

–Bob Probert (1965–), Chicago Blackhawks left winger, to arresting officers in Chicago, after he had crashed his motorcycle into a car with a blood alcohol level that was more than three times the legal limit

What are you, the fight doctor now or something? You've never been in a fight in your life, so what are you talking about?

–Rob Ray (1968–), Buffalo Sabres right winger, to a reporter after Ray was pounded by Edmonton's Georges Laraque

We kind of looked at each other and said, "That was fun." It was a couple guys beating on each other. Good times.

> —Scott Parker (1978–), San Jose Sharks right winger, after fighting Columbus Blue Jackets left winger Jody Shelley

Matthew's got that fearless attitude…he can laugh at danger and laugh at any type of fear. He's a guy that can spark you at any time. He does everything. He agitates; he's a good playmaker.

> —Lindy Ruff (1960–), Buffalo Sabres head coach, on Sabres right winger Mathew Barnaby

There are certain things about my game I don't want to change, but I think it's about time that I realized I can't fight every battle. Three hundred minutes in penalties is way too many. Way too many.

> —Rick Tocchet (1964–), Philadephia Flyer right winger

I had a poster of Probert on my wall. When I fought him for the first and only time, I though to myself, "Great, I got out alive."

> —Eric Cairns (1974–), New York Islanders defenseman, on fighting Bob Probert, reputed to be the toughest enforcer in the NHL

The truth is I would never spit on somebody. I would punch him first.

> —Martin Lapointe (1973–), Detroit Red Wings right winger, on an accusation that he, teammate Steve Yzerman and head coach Scotty Bowman assaulted a cameraman

HOCKEY VIOLENCE

Part of the drama and the excitement of NHL hockey, one has to admit, is its violence. Since the beginning, hard checks and aggressive play have been what the fans want and what the players love. It just wouldn't be hockey without the rough stuff.

Without violence, there would be no such thing as hockey.

–Clarence Campbell (1905–84), NHL president

Violence is what keeps the game alive.

–Harold Ballard (1903–90), Toronto Maple Leafs owner

Good hockey should be a game of speed, stick-handling and skating. If people want violence, they should go to the wrestling matches.

–Fred "Cyclone" Taylor (1884–1979),
Vancouver Millionaires forward

You want to call that violence? We call it action!

–George "Punch" Imlach (1918–87), Toronto Maple Leafs head coach, at the assault trial of Red Wings left winger Dan Maloney for his 1975 attack on Maple Leafs defenseman Brian Glennie

Canadian hockey has been carried to all parts of the world, usually on a stretcher.

–Eric Nichol and Dave More in their book *The Joy of Hockey*

It felt like a golf swing, and my head was on the tee.

–Tyler Wright (1973–), Edmonton Oilers center, on being hit in the head by Chicago Blackhawk right winger Joe Murphy

We've got to stamp out that kind of thing, or people are going to keep on buying tickets.

> —Conn Smythe (1895–1980), Toronto Maple Leafs owner and hockey builder, after witnessing an on-ice fight between Maurice Richard and Bob Bailey

The NHL theory of violence is nothing more than original violence tolerated and accepted, in time turned into custom, into spectacle, into tactic and finally into theory.

> —Ken Dryden (1947–), Montréal Canadiens goaltender, in his book *The Game*

Canada offers the world a unique sporting spectacle—wrestling and boxing matches fought by men wearing ice skates. Ancient Rome would have loved it.

> —Richard J. Needham (1912–96), Toronto *Globe and Mail* columnist

Hockey is the only team sport in the world that actually encourages fighting. I have no idea why we let it go on. The game itself is so fast, so exciting, so much fun to watch, why do we have to turn ice red so often? Why do the best shots in a game have to be on somebody's nose instead of somebody's net?

> —Wayne Gretzky (1961–), NHL great

Violence in sports is father to violence in everyday life.

> —Sidney Harris, Ontario provincial court judge, upon sentencing Minnesota North Stars right winger Dino Ciccarelli for assault in 1988, the first time any NHL player was convicted of assault during a game

The Russians are the dirtiest players I've ever seen.

> —Bobby Clarke (1949–), Philadelphia Flyers center, on his experience in the 1972 Canada-U.S.S.R Summit Series

Lemieux fights like a girl. He couldn't beat his way out of
a paper bag.

> —John Muckler (1934–), New York Rangers coach, on New Jersey
> Devils right winger Claude Lemieux

Two people fighting is not violence in hockey. It might be in
tennis or bowling, but it's not in hockey.

> —Gerry Cheevers (1940–), Boston Bruins goaltender

The people who yell and scream about hockey violence are
a handful of intellectuals and newspapermen who never pay
to get in to see a game. The fans, who shell out the money,
have always liked good, rough hockey.

> —Don Cherry (1934–), Canadian hockey commentator

This is the most excited you can be as a hockey player. As
much as you hate a team like Colorado, you love to play'em.
The juices will be boiling, and the blood will be flowing. Let's
clarify that: flowing through your body, not on the ice.

> —Kris Draper (1971–), Detroit Red Wings center, about his team's
> rivalry with the Colorado Avalanche

It's going to be good [to be] on his side for a change. I'll save
a lot of energy since I don't have to concentrate on whacking
him. I'm pretty excited about that.

> —Doug Gilmour (1963–), Chicago Blackhawks forward, on playing
> with new teammate Chris Chelios

People are going to say what they're going to say, but when
someone steps on you with a skate, I don't think anyone
deserves that.

> —Ryan Kesler (1984–), Vancouver Canucks center, on the notion
> that his agitating style may have somehow provoked Chris Pronger's
> skate attack in a March 12, 2008, game against the Anaheim Ducks

I'm going to say, "Hey buddy, remember me, the guy whose career you almost ended last year? See this dent in my face? Want to be roomies?"

> –Todd Fedoruk (1979–), Minnesota Wild left winger, on being picked up on waivers in 2007 by Minnesota and becoming a teammate of Derek Boogaard, whose right hand broke Fedoruk's orbital bone in an October 27, 2006, fight

Hockey is a tough game. With all the talk and everything that's going on right now, it frightens me a little bit that we are giving our players an excuse not to hit. I just hope that we don't take that out of our game at the pro level.

> –Bobby Orr (1948–), Boston Bruins great

I don't know if high-sticking is up. I don't think so. Some of those old guys were pretty cut up. And you know, [current high-stick incidents] are all accidental. So I don't know how there could be more now compared to back then, where there were a lot more intentional ones, for sure. There were some wicked stickmen when I started. It was part of it. That's how guys like Bobby Schmautz played, and even Wayne Cashman, who was a helluva stickman. And guys were proud of it. It was, "Hey, if you screw around with me, I'm gonna carve your eyes out." There's an expression you never hear any more.

> –Craig MacTavish (1958–), Edmonton Oilers head coach

He just got me in the right spot, in the small of the back. A good, clean, dirty hit...not that I didn't deserve it.

> –Chris Chelios (1962–), Detroit Red Wings defenseman, after taking a hit from Calgary Flames defensemen Glen Featherstone

REDUNDANCY

Hockey players like to make sure things are clear, even if that means the explanation doesn't make any sense.

Better teams win more often than the teams that are not so good.

> –Tom Watt (1935–), Maple Toronto Maple Leafs head coach

I'll be sad to go, and I wouldn't be sad to go. It wouldn't upset me to leave St. Louis, but it would upset me to leave St. Louis. It's hard to explain. You'll find out one of these days, but maybe you never will.

> –Brett Hull (1964–), St. Louis Blues right winger,
> on a possible trade

I love to play for Pittsburgh. If they can't afford me, then I'd love to play in L.A. or New York.

> –Jaromir Jágr (1972–), Pittsburgh Penguins right winger

It's not so much maturity as it is growing up.

> –Jay Miller (1960–), Boston Bruins left winger, when asked if his
> improved play was due to his maturity

I have never seen myself play.

> –Doug Harvey (1924–89), Montréal Canadiens defenseman, when
> asked by a reporter if he could rate his own playing

Half the game is mental; the other half is being mental.

> –Jim McKenny (1946–), Toronto Maple Leafs defenseman

The worst thing you can do is overreact. But it's also not good to underreact either.

> —Lou Lamoriello (1942–), New Jersey Devils general manager

Guys, I don't want to tell you half-truths, unless they're completely accurate.

> —Alain Vigneault (1961–), Montréal Canadiens head coach

Daneyko got mad when Kaminski said he was going to knock his teeth out. Dano has only two teeth left, so you can't say that to Dano.

> —Jacques Lemaire (1945–), New Jersey Devils head coach,
> on the Ken Daneyko–Kevin Kaminski feud

HEALTH, INJURIES AND RECOVERY

Serious injury is a constant risk in a sport as physical as hockey. Goalies now wear masks, and players wear helmets, but the true NHL player knows he is going to get battered sometime and puts his best face on it.

We get nose jobs all the time in the NHL, and we don't even have to go to the hospital.

—Brad Park (1948–), Detroit Red Wings defenseman

I was 14 when I lost them [his front teeth]. The main thing was we won that game, so I was the happiest. You hate to lose your teeth and the game, too.

—Bill Barber (1952–), Philadelphia Flyers left winger

The thing about playing at this age, it's like playing injured all the time. If I dyed my hair, they'd want more speed.

—Gordie Howe (1928–), Detroit Red Wings great, who retired from the NHL at the age of 52

There is no such thing as painless goaltending. If they could get enough padding to assure against every type of bruise, you'd have to be swung into position with a small derrick.

—Don Cherry (1934–), Canadian hockey commentator

It's no big deal. Like Gordie Howe says, elbows are to hockey players what fenders are to cars.

—Eric Lindros (1973–), Philadelphia Flyers center, after injuring his elbow

Man that guy is ripped! I mean I've got the washboard stomach, too. It's just that mine has about two months of laundry on top of it.

—Shawn Burr (1966–), Detroit Red Wings center, on Eric Lindros

Everybody says your health is the most important thing, and he's a perfect example. If he would have been healthy, he would have broken a lot of records. Maybe not all of them, but I'm pretty sure a lot of them. He was the best player I've ever seen. He was the most gifted at everything—size, strength, skill, how smart he was. There is no other player like him.

—Jaromir Jágr (1972–), Pittsburgh Penguins right winger, on teammate Mario Lemieux

You just weren't hugged enough as a child. That's why you've got issues.

—Hal Gill (1975–), Pittsburgh Penguins defenseman, to New York Rangers left winger Sean Avery during the 2008 playoffs

One good thing is that when I forget something, maybe I could tell my wife that it's brain damage.

—Murray Eaves (1960–), Detroit Red Wings forward, after receiving his second concussion in three months

If I get run into again, I'm taking someone with me. I lost one knee. I'll take a head if it happens again.

—Grant Fuhr (1962–), Edmonton Oilers goaltender, on the dangers of tending goal

I just tape four Tylenols to it.

—Boris Mironov (1972–), New York Rangers defenseman, on playing with a sore ankle

We start out with goalies wearing masks. Every club has a defenseman or two who goes down to smother shots. Soon, they'll want masks. All forwards will wear helmets. The team will become faceless, headless robots, all of whom look alike to the spectators. We can't afford to take that fan appeal away from hockey.

—Murray "Muzz" Patrick (1916–98), New York Rangers defenseman

Getting cut in the face is a real pain in the butt.

—Theoren Fleury (1968–), Calgary Flames right winger

Wrapping Christmas presents is tough. Even peeling a Mandarin orange is tough. I have to get my kids to help me.

—Brendan Morrison (1975–), Vancouver Canucks center, on wearing a cast on his right wrist after the surgery that cut his NHL ironman streak short at 542 games

You know what they say, "Behind every good man, there's a great woman." Not that I'm saying I'm a good man.

—Sandis Ozoliņš (1972–), San Jose Sharks defenseman, on the support he's gotten from his wife Sandra in his fight against alcoholism and his return to the NHL

I tried to get away, but he still found me. I told the trainers that he has a GPS in his stick to find my ankle bone.

—Niclas Havelid (1973–), Atlanta Thrashers defenseman, on how Washington Capitals sniper Alexander Ovechkin keeps hitting him with shots on the power play

One was on the ice, and we put that one back in. Another was up my nose, and they had to pull it down.

—Sami Kapanen (1973–), Philadelphia Flyers right winger, on how his front teeth were salvaged after being knocked out in 1998

Pain is nothing. Pain is in the mind. If you can walk you can run.

–Cam Neely (1965–), Boston Bruins right winger

It must be the body. It's chiseled out of marshmallows.

–Tony Amonte (1970–), Calgary Flames right winger, on possessing the NHL's second-longest active playing streak

I mean, the best thing for my knee, for anyone's knee, is to never play again and retire. But I'm not going to do that.

–Steve Yzerman (1965–), Detroit Red Wings center, preparing to hobble through another Stanley Cup run

I think helmets are extremely dangerous. They have never designed one specifically for a child. They are too big and too cumbersome. Kids perceive they are protected, and they are not. Everyone thinks it is common sense that they're good, but they're not.

–Derek Sanderson (1946–), Boston Bruins center, on not letting his kids near the rink

Eric dropped the gloves, and I said, "I'll fight you, but my hit was legal. You had your head down. You have to keep your head up." I don't think he got hurt then because he stayed in the game, and I know I didn't hurt him during the fight. I hope he's back real soon. He's a great player and this game needs him.

–Jason Doig (1977–), Washington Capitals defenseman, after handing Eric Lindros his eighth concussion

People break their face all the time. It's part of the job.

–Todd Fedoruk, (1979–), Minnesota Wild left winger, after surgery

In instances like this, it might make sense if the player is suspended indefinitely until you get more information back on the extent of the injury. That's one way you could address the situation. We know this is a dangerous game...a physical game, a speed game. But there are lines that shouldn't be crossed.

–John Ferguson Jr. (1967–), Toronto Maple Leafs general manager, on a questionable hit by New Jersey Devils Cam Janssen on Leafs defenseman Tomáš Kaberle

There was no blinding light, no angels coming to take me home. Everyone tells me how concerned they were for me, but I don't remember much of that. When I woke up, I thought about Mother's Day, and then, when I saw Al MacInnis standing over me, praying, all I could remember were those many stories Al tells me about lobster traps and how he unloaded them for pocket change on the docks in Nova Scotia when he was growing up.

–Chris Pronger (1974–), St. Louis Blues defenseman, on the moments after he was hit in the heart with a slapshot during the 1998 playoffs against the Detroit Red Wings

At least I don't need a mask for Halloween now.

–Andreas Dackell (1972–), Montréal Canadiens right winger, after suffering facial cuts that required 30 stitches

AFTER ALL, IT IS A BUSINESS

If players and owners cannot find a way to make money, there will be no more hockey. The challenges of the modern media age and the megasalaries being offered to coaches and players alike means that there is more to keeping the game alive than just getting the puck in the net.

We have organized to promote and protect the best interests of the players. We don't intend to start a revolution. We aren't displeased or discontented about a single thing.

–Ted Lindsay (1925–), Detroit Red Wings left winger, on the attempted formation of a NHL players union in the 1950s

I wouldn't ever go into a season trying to rebuild from scratch. You can't trade good players for high picks because the world ends at the end of each season. Live with the idea that the world is flat, and you're coming to the edge.

–Neil Smith (1955–), New York Rangers general manager

I don't want to talk about today's market anymore because nobody can make sense of what the market is. It's all over the map. There's a bunch of lunatics out there throwing money away. I'm sick and tired of it. It's lunacy. Punch me in the head and tell me I'm stupid, but that's the way I feel. There's no sense to it anymore.

–Kevin Lowe (1959–), Edmonton Oilers general manager

The National Hockey League is a business. Its business is entertainment. The entertainment it presents is sport.

–John A. Ziegler, Jr. (1934–), NHL president

At the request of the Maple Leaf Gardens, we have omitted the toy or prize inside this box of Cracker Jack, as anything thrown on the ice may cause serious injury to a player

—Notice printed inside each box of Cracker Jack candied popcorn sold in Maple Leaf Gardens after fans threw most of the prizes onto the ice

"Sports" had become "Sports Inc." With big money now to be made in sports, big money would be made, and the attitude changed. "Cities" became "markets," "games" became "products," "sports" part of the "entertainment business," fighting for "entertainment dollars."

—Ken Dryden (1947–), Montréal Canadiens Hall of Fame goaltender, from his best-selling book *The Game*

Contracts are broken every day by everybody around, including those people who open the biggest mouths in Canada, including the ownership of the Ottawa Senators. Where is the sanctity of the guaranteed contract when you can hide behind bankruptcy?

—Mark Gandler, agent for New York Islanders center Alexei Yashin, on news that Yashin might never see the money owed to him by the bankrupt Ottawa Senators.

As a rule, if there are any rules in this business, you don't want them to be too bright at anything but hockey. If they have little outside interest, and their minds aren't occupied elsewhere, they're more likely to concentrate on the game. A man may be almost illiterate, he may be unable to hold a responsible job, but by some queer quirk that I can't understand, he may have the best hockey brains in the game. But what makes hockey brains, where they come from or how they work, no one knows.

—Lester Patrick (1883–1960), NHL player, coach and general manager

There's great growth in hockey. In the way hockey is shot [on television], we can be creative in creating stars. We do it in the movie business.

–Michael Eisner (1942–), Walt Disney Company CEO

The new realities of the hockey industry, the size of the Québec City market and the absence of adequate government help sounded the [death] knell of the Nordiques.

–Marcel Aubut (1948–), Québec Nordiques president

For a purely business transaction, the NHL is too big for Winnipeg. I think everybody knows that.

–Barry Shenkarow, Winnipeg Jets owner and president

I don't know the salaries of the other players, and I really don't want to know. It's the World Hockey Association, I think, that was the direct cause to all the changes in salary structures. But I think that the excesses are over and that soon things will be back to normal.

–Yvan Cournoyer (1943–), Montréal Canadiens right winger, on NHL salaries in the 1970s

The three important elements of hockey are forecheck, backcheck and paycheck.

–Gil Perreault (1950–), Buffalo Sabres center

We're looking forward to building the type of team the Rangers are able to buy.

–Bobby Smith (1958–), Phoenix Coyotes general manager

Bob Goodenow will kill me, but if we're going to be realistic about things, probably 75 percent of the league is overpaid. But we're not paying ourselves. There are people giving it to us, and no one is putting a gun to their heads. Something has to be done if we're going to fix this. I don't think there can be a stoppage. I don't think the game can afford it, especially in Canada where it's vital we at least have this many teams up here.

–Brett Hull (1964–), St. Louis Blues right winger,
on the NHL salary crunch

I have to thank the guy who fired me because he was also the guy who hired me.

–Serge Savard (1946–), Montréal Canadiens general manager,
on his firing from Montréal

My plan was that when we start winning, we will fill this building. It's the only thing I haven't been able to do. And I don't want to hear that price is an issue. We have one of the lowest average prices in the NHL, and we've already run every kind of special. About the only thing we haven't done is a "buy in the next 30 minutes, and the GM will wash your car" deal.

–Jay Feaster (1962–), Tampa Bay Lightning general manager,
taking a swipe at the locals

I cannot go along with the policy of the present management to put cash ahead of class!

–Conn Smythe (1895–1980), Toronto Maple Leafs owner and
hockey builder, after handing over the Maple Leafs to
Harold Ballard

THE NHL LOCKOUT

The lesson of lockouts? Everyone loses.

I'm ashamed by what we did. Smart people should have solved this by today.

> –Tim Leiweke, Los Angeles Kings president,
> on the 2004–05 lockout

There is no money in Germany. There's no money, other than with a few teams, in Switzerland. The players may think, "Well, let's all go to Europe," but I can tell the guys, there's not a lot of opportunity here. There's no real solution in Europe in terms of jobs because, if you look at the salary they can make and what they have to insure themselves for to cover their NHL futures, they actually don't make any money. They're playing for their per diems.

> –Dave King (1947–), Hamburg (Germany) Freezers head coach,
> on players working in Europe during the NHL lockout season

We want the right deal. The hockey's not important.

> –Jim Devellano, Detroit Red Wings senior vice-president

The hypocrisy of it is unbelievable. They don't want a salary cap, but they'll come to a league that has a salary cap and take someone else's job. I make $700 a week, and I have a wife and two kids and a mortgage payment. Here I wish I could play in the NHL for a fraction of what they make, and here they're going to come play in our league for $500 a week. It's really bizarre.

> –Kevin Kerr (1967–), Flint Generals right winger, on locked-out
> Red Wings Chris Chelios, Derian Hatcher and Kris Draper,
> who joined the Motor City Mechanics of the UHL

I think the biggest thing I learned is that I probably shouldn't use the word *never* as much as I did. Ultimately we have a cap, and guys like me said we never would have one, so maybe we're eating our words in some sense.

—Scott Walker (1973–), Carolina Hurricanes right winger

I think that there are a number of fans in this country who have sensed over the last number of months that actually, maybe, it was more habit than it was passion. I think for the great majority, it's still a passion. But others have discovered that maybe it was something else. And so, as much as this can be problematic in the U.S., and that's where it's usually talked about, I think it's also a problem in this country.

—Ken Dryden (1947–), Montréal Canadiens Hall of Fame goaltender, on the erosion of fan support for the NHL

At the end of the 301-day lockout, it can accurately be said that many NHL owners wanted to destroy Executive Director Bob Goodenow and the militant wing of the NHL Players Association. And they were willing to spend billions to do so. So they did.

—Bruce Dowbiggin, writer and sports journalist

There are 700 guys trying to call one number, trying to talk to Bob [NHL Players Association Executive Director Bob Goodenow]. My feeling is I'm confused and disappointed. I thought the players were tougher on this.

—Brad Lukowich (1976–), Tampa Bay Lightning defenseman

Why did we sit out all year to do this?

—Turner Stevenson (1972–), Philadelphia Flyers right winger

Am I mad? No. I want to get back to work. But at the same time, I'm just a little disappointed that it went this far to play poker and to have someone call your bluff.

—Matthew Barnaby (1973–), Chicago Blackhawks right winger

The game's just suffered an absolute blow it'll never recover from. They're totally underestimating the damage that's been done. I'm just really disappointed and, to be honest with you, I'm embarrassed to be a player in the NHL.

—Rod Brind'Amour (1970–), Carolina Hurricanes center

I'm sick when we go around to the restaurants. Some of the managers get mad at me: "When are you playing? When are you playing?" I don't blame them. It's devastating for them.

—Doug MacLean (1954–), Columbus Blue Jackets president

In the old days, you could have a guy who couldn't do anything but fight because he wouldn't hurt you too much on the ice. But with the up-and-down of the game now, you have to be able to do more than fight. Plus, with the salary cap, you can't afford to keep around guys who fight and don't do much else. You watch. In a couple of seasons, there will hardly be any fights at all. That's where the game is headed.

—Phil Esposito (1942–), Boston Bruins great

The owners are the ones who gave away the money. If nobody's going to give you that, you're not going to sign it. They're all mad at the players, but players didn't write those contracts up.

—Robert Lang (1970–), Chicago Blackhawks center

If the owners are playing a high-stakes game of chicken, they'd be better off playing it with anybody else in the world besides hockey players. Because of all sports, we're probably the most stubborn, pig-headed players.

—Scott Walker (1973–), Carolina Hurricanes right winger

I don't blame the players; they're just doing what they do. The union should have addressed this, though. They should have shown some direction. It's not right what they're doing. If it wasn't [for the lockout] I'd still be there playing. I know that. A lot of guys have lost jobs; a lot of guys are sitting out watching NHL guys play in their place....I can tell you that right now. If they want me to be a replacement player, I'll play.

—Lonny Bohonos (1973–), Chicago Wolves center,
on the NHL lockout

Gary Bettman has put the league in this situation. A guy who doesn't do his job shouldn't be there....Hockey's not a national sport in the U.S., and Gary Bettman doesn't have a feel for that. That's my opinion. There's a lot of players— especially a lot of guys that come over from Europe—who are average players....It's a business, and you take chances. Nothing's guaranteed in business. Teams come and go. You saw what happened to Minnesota. You see what happened to Cleveland in football. One of the best football cities there ever was, with the history in Cleveland, and they lost their team for a couple years. So that's just the nature of the beast. If some teams have to go or you can't make it, then so be it. The players aren't going to feel it as much as the owners.

—Chris Chelios (1962–), Detroit Red Wings defenseman

What will happen with the new system is the inflationary pressure caused by the inflation in player costs will be abated. What happens in each market will be a club-by-club decision. But I do believe the ticket situation, the pricing situation, will be improved and will be more reflective of a healthy business.

–Gary Bettman (1952–), NHL commissioner, acknowledging that a new collective bargaining agreement cannot guarantee lower NHL ticket prices

As I stand before you today, it is my sad duty to announce…it no longer is practical to conduct even an abbreviated season.

–Gary Bettman (1952–), NHL commissioner, on the cancellation of the 2004–05 season

Everybody out there who calls us spoiled because we play "a game," they can all kiss my ass. They can all kiss my ass because we have tried so hard to get this game back on the ice.

–Jeremy Roenick, (1970–), San Jose Sharks center, on the 2004–05 lockout

I go from locker to locker, pretending the guys are here. You know, give them a little bit of a pep talk. It must be working, because we haven't lost a game yet.

–Tom McVie (1935–), Boston Bruins assistant coach, talking about his activities during the 1994–95 lockout

STRATEGY AND WORDS OF WISDOM

*Football has Vince Lombardi. Baseball has Yogi Berra.
Hard acts to follow, but hockey tries its best.*

By the 1980s, the amount of line juggling had increased to
the point where you never could predict the combination that
would be used by the other team, and a coach had to make
quick changes—sometimes just one player—to try and nul-
lify what the other team was trying. Since then, a pattern has
been for two players to be linemates over the long haul with
a variety of mates in the third slot, depending on the situation.

–Glen Sather (1943–), Edmonton Oilers head coach

I wanted somebody on the other team to make me work
harder. When somebody was checking me closely I wanted to
get away from him, and I tried all the more to get my goals.
If I didn't have anyone on my back or anybody to check me,
I don't think I would have accomplished all that I did.

–Maurice Richard (1921–2000), Montréal Canadiens great

Our system of forechecking is to shoot the puck and leave
it there.

–Harry Neale (1937–), Vancouver Canucks head coach

When I saw the skill and intelligence they had on the ice,
I volunteered to play their style and forget about mine.

–Bobby Hull (1939–), Winnipeg Jets left winger, on playing with
the European players on the Jets

When we've got the puck, they can't score.

–Paul Coffey (1961–), Edmonton Oilers defenseman

If everyone elevates their game by 2 percent with Mats gone, that equals 40 percent.

> —Curtis Joseph (1967–), Toronto Maple Leafs goaltender, on how his team might respond to losing captain Mats Sundin after the 2007–08 season

They were checking us so closely, I could tell what brand of deodorant they were using.

> —Gary Dornhoefer (1943–), Philadelphia Flyers right winger, after playing the Montréal Canadiens

Everyone says there is only the trap on this team, but there is a lot more. Go to hell with the trap.

> —Jacques Lemaire (1945–), Minnesota Wild head coach

If he hits you, he hurts you. We're gonna put three guys on him.

> —Lindy Ruff (1960–), Buffalo Sabres head coach

Good goaltenders will make me a good coach and that goes for anybody in the league.

> —Barry Trotz (1962–), Nashville Predators head coach

Many times, he pushed me so hard that I ended up crying. I would wonder why he was so mean to me, but I didn't understand what he was trying to do. He meant it in a good way.

> —Zdeno Chára (1977–), Boston Bruins defenseman, on learning the game from his father

At 16, I began playing for junior teams. I traveled abroad and came to believe that if you have an opportunity to see and get to know the world, it's stupid to waste your time doing nothing.

> —Sergei Gonchar (1974–), Pittsburgh Penguins defenseman

Forget about talent; worry about results.

> —Bobby Orr (1948–), Boston Bruins great

Now I see what I was doing wrong. I had learned only defensive skills, and what was most natural for me wasn't being developed.

> —Sergei Gonchar (1974–), Pittsburgh Penguins defenseman, on his first few years in the NHL

I did get a kick out of his philosophy. He was always saying when he was up in Bracebridge [his hometown], on the roof of a cottage and hammering a nail, that there aren't 15,000 people booing if he bends one. If you bend a nail, you bend a nail. He would hint that he couldn't take the pressure.

> —Dave Dryden (1941–), Buffalo Sabres goaltender, on his goaltending partner Roger Crozier's philosophical approach to the game

A goalie has to show he's confident, to his teammates as well as himself. You are the last guy before that special red line. You make yourself confident. You make yourself hard to beat.

> —Patrick Roy (1965–), Colorado Avalanche goaltender

We had to do two things: build an organization which on one hand could recruit the very best talent available right across Canada, and at the same time develop the pool of players in our backyard, Québec.

> —Frank Selke (1893–1985), Montréal Canadiens general manager, on rebuilding the team during the 1940s

Players today put too much emphasis on lifting weights, low body fat and big muscles that they think make them look good—all that bullsh**. What you need to play hockey is heart and determination, and the ability to stay mentally strong. Mental strength beats physical strength any day.

> —Phil Esposito (1942–), Boston Bruins great

TRADES AND CONTRACTS

*Players now seldom stay with the same team for life,
in fact they seldom have. These days, keeping track is
harder than ever.*

I just don't know what to think. I play in Colorado, they tell
me they like me, and I get traded. I play in Calgary, and at
the end of the season the GM tells me he likes me, and I get
traded. I just hope my fiancée doesn't tell me she likes me.

> –Chris Drury (1976–), Buffalo Sabres left winger, on being traded
> so often. He now plays for the New York Rangers.

The last three weeks have been a whirlwind for my wife and
myself. But this was my own gut feeling and my own decision. I am disappointed in having to leave Edmonton.
[Crying]. I promised "Mess" I wouldn't do this.

> –Wayne Gretzky (1961–), NHL great, on his 1988 trade to the Los
> Angeles Kings

He's a great actor. I though he pulled it off beautifully when
he showed how upset he was, but he wants the big dream.

> –Peter Pocklington (1943–), Edmonton Oilers owner, on the
> Wayne Gretzky trade press conference

The only difference between the Coyotes and *Days of Our
Lives* is that nobody has been shot on our team yet.

> –Jeremy Roenick (1970–), Phoenix Coyotes center, on the trade
> rumors in 2001 surrounding Coyotes captain Keith Tkachuk.
> Tkachuk ended up being traded to the St. Louis Blues.

There's no bloody way he wanted to go. He's a small town guy.

–Paul Coffey (1961–), Edmonton Oilers defenseman,
on the Wayne Gretzky trade

I've got to do something radical to sell hockey in L.A., and there's no name in hockey like Wayne Gretzky.

–Bruce McNall (1950–), Los Angeles Kings owner

Wayne wouldn't let Edmonton, fans, Canada, and, most important, his teammates down without good reason. Pocklington is the reason Wayne is gone.

–Janet Gretzky (1961–), Wayne Gretzky's wife

There is no price on greatness. They'd have my head if I sold him.

–Peter Pocklington (1943–), Edmonton Oilers owner, on Wayne Gretzky in an interview on March 31, 1980. He traded Gretzky to the Los Angeles Kings in 1988.

I couldn't cope with his nonsense any more. He was driving me nuts, always something wrong with him.

–Hector "Toe" Blake (1912–95), Montréal Canadiens head coach, on goaltender Jacques Plante's trade

It's not about the money. It's about what I believe in.

–Sergei Fedorov (1969–), Detroit Red Wings center, on holding out for $6.5 million from the Red Wings in 1998

It's beyond money at this point. They're not even treating him as a member of their family, unless it's a dysfunctional family.

–Kurt Overhardt, agent to Brendan Morrison, during contract negotiations with the New Jersey Devils

When you ask for the house, car, cat, dog and all the fish when you're dealing with a player who's got questions about his health, no GM in his right mind is going to say yes and offer to clean the aquarium too.

—Eric Lindros (1973–), Philadelphia Flyers center, on the inability of Flyers general manager Bobby Clarke to trade him

I had fun playing the game, and the Blackhawks brass thought I should be more serious about it. We finished first for the first time in the team's history in the 1966–67 season and had a little party to celebrate. I drank too much champagne and got brave. I told Tommy Ivan, "We have a dynasty here. Don't screw it up!" After we lost the first round of the playoffs to Toronto, and I didn't have a point in six games, I was gone.

—Phil Esposito (1942–), Boston Bruins great, on the real reason he got traded to the Bruins

Anybody that doesn't think the organization did the right thing by trading Pavel, if they spent five minutes in the dressing room, they wouldn't be speaking negatively about the trade. Everyone that's been around him knows what he brings to the table—that's goals, and that's it.

—Trevor Kidd (1972–), Florida Panthers goaltender, on the 2002 trade that sent right winger Pavel Bure from the Panthers to the New York Rangers

I got traded for a dollar, you know. And here I am sitting in Team Canada's dressing room at the World Cup. It's unbelievable.

—Kris Draper (1971–), Detroit Red Wings center, contemplates his path from Winnipeg to the 2004 World Cup. The Jets had sold Draper to Detroit for one dollar in 1993.

I don't really think about the contract right now. I just think about my game and what I have to do better, and that's it.

—Alexander Ovechkin (1985–), Washington Capitals left winger, on contract talks with the Capitals

You could take a stat of every high-scoring free agent that signed with another team and what he did in the first year there, and I guarantee you, it's not very good. And the only reason it's not very good is because it's very hard in a short period of time for players to make an emotional connection to the team. We saw that with [Brett] Hull and [Pat] Verbeek in Dallas. They didn't have the season they had the year before, but in the second year they were connected. You're expecting Robert Lang or Jágr and those players to step right in, but it's difficult. Everything is new to them—the way you practice and train, the way the coaches talk between periods. Everything is foreign. And scoring players—it's different if the guy is a role player—have to feel comfortable. And if you don't feel comfortable, then you're not emotionally con- nected, and that takes time.

—Ken Hitchcock (1951–), Philadelphia Flyers head coach

I was fighting back tears, so I could only imagine what Mark was going through. You really feel what Mark meant to the city and what the city meant to him. How could anyone watch that and not feel emotional? He brought their team the Stanley Cup. Thank God he's on our team now.

—Dave Scatchard (1976–), Vancouver Canucks center, on Mark Messier's first game in New York's Madison Square Garden after his 1997 trade to the Canucks from the New York Rangers

Now we've got men 6'1" who look small. Now a guy like Marty [McSorley] doesn't even stand out on the ice, except for his beautiful blond hair.

—Barry Melrose (1956–), Los Angeles Kings head coach, describing his 1994–95 team

I'd rather play against Claude Lemieux four times a year than play against Wendel or Steve Thomas four times a year.

> —Pat Burns (1952–), New Jersey Devils head coach, on the three-way trade involving Steve Thomas, Wendel Clark and Claude Lemieux

[Roberta] was scheduled to undergo major surgery June 22, and I didn't feel it was appropriate to sign until I knew everything was in order. So I put it on hold. Meanwhile, all these reports going around were erroneous and disappointing. No one knows what my family has gone through recently, but at least my wife is on the road to recovery. It's very difficult to deal with these issues while your family is being ripped in the press.

> —Bryan McCabe (1975–), Toronto Maple Leafs defenseman, on the difficulty of dealing with the re-signing of his contract with Toronto Maple Leafs during the off-season

I'm a lot happier that he's on my team.

> —Marián Hossa (1979–), Ottawa Senators right winger, on his new teammate Zdeno Chára arriving in 2001

Hartford isn't exactly a media hotbed either, so you don't really get the correlation of the two cities and you don't get to read about other players, whether it be from St. Louis or other areas. So I didn't realize the type of respect and the type of player Brendan had become here in St. Louis. You know he scored 50 goals and all those things, but you don't realize what a pillar of the community he was and the things that he did off the ice that everybody loved him for.

> —Chris Pronger (1974–), Detroit Red Wings defenseman, on new teammate Brendan Shanahan's 1996 trade from the Hartford Whalers

I think the trade just gave me a chance to reflect and realize that things are never as bad as you might think, that you just can't be too hard on yourself.

–Eric Brewer (1979–), Edmonton Oilers defenseman, on being traded from the New York Islanders to the Oilers in 2000

Even if you would give us the entire Leafs team, and even Maple Leaf Gardens, the answer would still be no!

–Frank Selke (1893–1985), Montréal Canadiens general manager, after he was asked by Toronto Maple Leafs owner Conn Smythe to trade Maurice Richard to the Leafs

At time he was such a problem, I wanted to send him down to Pittsburgh, but thank God we kept him!

–Conn Smythe (1895–1980), Toronto Maple Leafs owner and hockey builder, on Bill Barilko after he scored in overtime of game five of the 1951 Stanley Cup final against the Montréal Canadiens to take the Cup for Toronto

FANS

Hockey fans are unique: they are passionate, obsessed and die-hard, both to the grave and beyond.

In Toronto, it's easier if no one knows you're a Maple Leaf.

> —Borje Salming (1951–), Toronto Maple Leafs defenseman

He could rile up the Montréal fans in a hurry. God, I sometimes felt sorry for the man. He must have got a standing ovation when he went shopping.

> —Gordie Howe (1928–), Detroit Red Wings great, on Canadiens icon Maurice Richard

We appreciate all the fans that are here, but we really respect the five or six who stayed with us all year.

> —Jon Casey (1962–), Minnesota North Stars goaltender, after a difficult season.

He asked that Mr. Bettman and Mr. Goodenow know that they are "skunks" for denying him the pleasure of watching the NHL on TV this year. He also asked that Mr. Bettman step aside and give Wayne Gretzky the job that rightfully belongs to him.

> —From the obituary of Archie Bennitz, a hockey fan who died on January 19, 2005, at the age of 84. Bennitz had requested that a message to the NHL be included in his death notice

You can't believe how excited I am because I missed it terribly. It's one of the greatest sports no one knows about.

> —Paul Brehne, New Jersey Devils fan, on hockey's return after the 2004–05 lockout season.

Nyet, nyet, Soviet! Da, da, Canada!

> —Canadian fans chant during the Summit Series.

Les Canadiens sont là!

> —Chant of Montréal Canadiens fans

Hey, New York Islanders, where were you the night we played the Rangers? We, your loyal fans showed up! We braved freezing weather and came out looking for a great game. We came out to support you. Where was the energy, the excitement, the electricity, the intensity? Come on now... we deserve a better effort. It's a tough road ahead. Your fans are behind you...play with passion!!! Let's Go Islanders! Signed, A Loyal Fan of the Team.

> —Larry Weinberger, an Islanders season-ticket holder, paid $28,000 for an ad in *New York Newsday* after watching his team lose 5–0 to the Rangers

Now I Can Die In Peace!

> —Sign held up by a New York Rangers fan after they won the Stanley Cup in 1994, their first Cup win in 54 years.

Your Honor, I was simply taking the Stanley Cup back to Montréal where it belongs.

> —Ken Kilander, Montréal Canadiens fan, to a judge after he was arrested for stealing the Stanley Cup from the 1961 champions Chicago Blackhawks

Sometimes you think they must have come out of the chimp cages at the Bronx Zoo.

> —Gerry Cheevers (1940–), Boston Bruins goaltender, on New York hockey fans

Those are the people you need the most…your home base
you expect to be with you. When they kind of turn on you,
it's just kind of like, well okay, we'll stick it up their ass too.

–Brett Hull, (1964–), Detroit Red Wings right winger, after the
Red Wings dropped the first two games of their opening round
series in Detroit against the Vancouver Canucks in the
2002 Stanley Cup finals and were booed off the ice by their
hometown fans

It's always been the policy of the Molson Centre, and prior
to that of the Forum, that signs are permitted at all events as
long as they don't convey a message that is in bad taste. It's
a judgment call, but having said that, we have very experienced
and very professional staff who deal with this type of situation every day. Security staff will sometimes remove signs if
they think it can become a source of friction between groups
of fans. We do it whether it's aimed at the Canadiens, the vis-
itors or anyone else.

–Donald Beauchamp, Montréal Canadiens spokesman, after a fan
was ordered to remove signs criticizing defenseman Patrice
Brisebois. The signs included the messages "Brise-boo" and
"$17 million waste."

Well, it is the silver anniversary, so I suppose it's fitting for
this to come up again now. It's unbelievable that after more
than 30 years in the game, pummeling a guy with his loafer
will be my legacy. But I guess it's better than having no legacy at all.

–Mike Milbury (1952–), New York Islanders general manager,
recalling December 23, 1979, when a brawl between the Bruins
and Rangers spread into the crowd. Milbury, then a Bruins forward, was seen whacking a fan with his own shoe

Only the Lord Saves More than Bernie Parent!

–Bumper sticker on Philadelphia Flyers fans cars

I was happy to have an attraction in our building that we didn't have to pay for.

> –Harold Ballard (1903–90), Toronto Maple Leafs owner,
> on a streaker in Maple Leaf Gardens

I think they bring me luck....I guess I'll have to like seafood now.

> –Patrick Roy (1965–), Colorado Avalanche goaltender,
> on the octopus-throwing Detroit Red Wing fans

I'm just glad it wasn't "Machete Night!"

> –Bob Froese (1958–), New York Rangers goaltender, when Ranger
> fans threw plastic mugs onto the ice after free mugs had been given
> to fans at the gates as part of "Mug Night"

They don't know a lick about hockey. They never leave in the third period because they think there's a fourth one.

> –Tom Fitzgerald (1968–), Nashville Predators right winger,
> on Nashville fans

COACHES

From "Toe" Blake to Don Cherry to Wayne Gretzky,
coaches in the NHL have never ceased to be inspiring,
colorful, and above all, hated.

When we're competing for the Stanley Cup, this record won't mean a thing.

> —Rick Bowness (1955–), Ottawa Senators head coach, after the Senators set an NHL record with 38 straight road losses in the 1992–93 season

Maybe one of the qualities of being a great coach is being a jerk. There are quite a few of them around.

> —Larry Robinson (1951–), New Jersey Devils head coach

This is my third time. They say you're not a coach in the league till you've been fired. I must be getting pretty good.

> —Terry Simpson (1943–), Winnipeg Jets head coach, after being fired

It's a great game. But coaches find a way to stop it.

> —Pat Quinn (1943–), Toronto Maple Leafs head coach, at a January 2005 summit meeting of coaches on the state of the game

Running the Buffalo club will be the toughest job in pro hockey. But, the tougher it is, the better I like it.

> —George "Punch" Imlach (1918–87), NHL coach and general manager, on taking the job as coach and general manager of the expansion Buffalo Sabres for the 1970–71 NHL season

There are two things I don't want to know: how they make hot dogs and what goes on in the NHL office.

—Roger Neilson (1934–2003), Ottawa Senators head coach

Coaches are like ducks. Calm on top, but paddling underneath. Believe me, there's a lot of leg movement.

—Ken Hitchcock (1951–), Columbus Blue Jackets head coach

There are three things that are sure: you're going to pay taxes, you're going to die and I'm going to change the lines.

—Pat Burns (1952–), New Jersey Devils head coach

Coaching the Bruins is like going bear hunting with a butter knife.

—Pat Burns (1952–), New Jersey Devils head coach

I know my players don't like my practices, but that's okay because I don't like their games.

—Harry Neale (1937–), Vancouver Canucks head coach

Listen fellas, I've got to tell you this. I'm not the greatest coach in the world. But if you look around this room you'll see that I don't have the greatest players either.

—Bernie "Boom Boom" Geoffrion (1931–2006),
New York Rangers head coach

You look like a monkey screwing a football.

—Herb Brooks (1937–2003), New York Rangers head coach,
to one of his players after a bad game

Your playing gets worse and worse every day, and now you're playing like it's next week.

> —Herb Brooks (1937–2003), New York Rangers head coach

To be honest, I was a bit fearful of whether I'd have [the coaching passion] when I started, but it's fired up again. I've trained hard to look after myself, and physically I feel strong.

> —Mike Keenan (1949–), Calgary Flames head coach, on his return to the NHL coaching ranks with the Flames

You know what, coaching is coaching. I got hired here to be me.

> —Brent Sutter (1962–), New Jersey Devils head coach, on implementing his own coaching philosophy with the Devils

There are still two or three guys who aren't willing to pay the price to win a game. This is not Wal-Mart. There are no discounts in this league.

> —Ron Wilson (1955–), San Jose Sharks head coach

It's like being coached by Red Auerbach or Bear Bryant. These are people who only came along once in a lifetime and to say he was your coach....It's hard to put into words.

> —Brett Hull (1964–), Detroit Red Wings right winger, after the Red Wings won the Stanley Cup, and head coach Scotty Bowman announced his retirement

When I broke into professional hockey at 17, I was told that I was too small and too slow, and I wouldn't make the NHL. Now it's kind of flip-flopped, and the sense is I can't be a good coach because I was a great athlete.

> —Wayne Gretzky (1961–), NHL great, on being Phoenix Coyotes head coach

People think there is something wrong with Mike. But there's method in his madness.

> —Scott Lachance (1972–), New York Islanders defenseman,
> describing New York Islanders head coach Mike Milbury

I would be sitting there, thinking about [Keenan] and how I wanted to kill him....In my mind, I'd be cutting his eyes out with my stick.

> —Brett Hull (1964–), St. Louis Blues right winger,
> on Blues coach Mike Keenan

The second-best thing about being hired by the Boston Bruins was that I'd finally made it as a coach in the NHL. The first best thing was that I was coach of the team for which Bobby Orr was a player. Mind you I didn't say that I'd coached Bobby Orr because that would be the most presumptuous thing any coach could ever say. He was the greatest hockey player I have ever seen, Gordie Howe and Wayne Gretzky included.

> —Don Cherry (1934–), Canadian hockey commentator and former
> Boston Bruins head coach

Joel was the perfect coach for me. As a former NHL defenseman, he, too, knew how to pick out the things I needed to improve on and how to get me to that point.

> —Chris Pronger (1974–), St. Louis Blues defenseman, on being
> a player under Blues head coach Joel Quenneville

The guy knew how to prime you for a game; he knew what button to push to get the most out of guys, because he always wanted to maintain the edge.

> —Jacques Plante (1929–86), Montréal Canadiens goaltender, on
> Canadiens head coach Hector "Toe" Blake

I remember that he would close the dressing room door after
a bad game and raise the roof in there. But when that door
opened to the media, you never heard a bad word from him
about any of his players. That kind of class will keep you in
white shirts for a long time.

—Red Storey (1918–2006), NHL referee, on Montréal Canadiens
coach Hector "Toe" Blake

I was playing the kids a lot, and after game five Henri, who
had been sitting on the bench a lot, blasted me. He said I was
a bad coach. Then the Forum started getting phone calls with
bomb threats. Remember this was after the Kidnap Crisis
and the War Measures Act, and French-English relations
were not so good.

—Al MacNeil (1935–), Montréal Canadiens head coach, on bench-
ing fan favorite Henri Richard in the early 1970s

Coaching offensively is too hard. You can give them a plan
of attack, and then the situation for the plan may never come
up in the game. But defense, now, think of all six men on the
ice doing the job on defense. I told my players if they worked
as hard coming back as they did going down the ice, we'd be
okay. Of course, you had to have the proper type of player to
handle that approach—or make them into the proper type.

—Clarence Henry "Hap" Day (1901–90),
Toronto Maple Leafs head coach

I've said this before, but it's really true: you have to get players
to do what they don't want to do.

—Ken Hitchcock (1951–), Columbus Blue Jackets head coach

REFEREES, RULES AND REGULATIONS

Even a seemingly free-for-all game like hockey has rules and referees to enforce them. Keeping order on the ice is a challenge not for the faint-hearted, though, and sometimes even the refs appreciate the comedy that some players produce in trying to get away with murder.

There's no question if someone's in trouble—or if a 6'4" guy is beating the sh** out of a guy 5'9". With two big guys, if they slow down you ask: "Have you had enough?" If they say no you just let 'em go. If they say yes, or nod, you step in. They have a job to do, but they don't want to kill each other. In March 1990, [Detroit's] Bob Probert broke my nose in a fight with [Chicago's] Bob McGill. He just kept whaling, and my blood was everywhere.

—Gerard Gauthier, NHL linesman, on the right time to
break up a fight

I saw courage last night. There were calls that haven't been made in 25 years.

—Stephen Walkom (1963–), NHL director of officials, reviews the
refereeing on opening night of the 2005–06 season under new
NHL guidelines

Everybody keeps saying this is great. It's not great. It's not hockey.…There are penalties all over.…There has to be some discretion. The referees have to use some judgment on what is a penalty and what is not.

—Steve Yzerman (1965–), Detroit Red Wings center, on the new
NHL regulations in the 2005–06 season

I think the game has gotten better. [The two-referee system] keeps players from taking cheap shots behind the play. I never thought I'd like it, considering the way I like to hack.

—Brian Skrudland (1963–), Dallas Stars center

Get used to this phrase: how could both referees have missed that?

—Mike Brophy, senior writer for *The Hockey News*, on the new two-referee experiment in 1998

That's a 12-year-old's goal pad, and that's illegal. It's tough to comment on these changes. If that pad I showed you is illegal on a 12-year-old, where do I start? Honestly, I think if they want to score more goals, they should take away our helmets.

—Trevor Kidd (1972–), Toronto Maple Leafs goaltender, displaying his son's pads to protest a 2004 rule limiting NHL goalie pads to 10 inches wide

I hate to tell you this son, but the pool is frozen over.

—Don Koharski (1955–), NHL referee, to Philadelphia Flyers left winger Bill Barber after Barber took an obvious dive

Have another doughnut, you fat pig.

—Jim Schoenfeld (1952–), New Jersey Devils head coach, to referee Don Koharski after a 1988 Stanley Cup playoff game in which Schoenfeld believed Koharski missed a few important calls

She might as well put on their jersey.

—Geraldine Heaney (1967–), Team Canada defenseman, after American referee Stacey Livingston called 12 penalties against Canada in the women's gold-medal game at the 2002 Winter Olympics

REFEREES, RULES AND REGULATIONS

Now when you're on the ice, you just go non-stop, and it's
hard. You come off the ice completely winded. Playing
hockey is fun. Going out and hooking and holding isn't fun.
People shouldn't confuse fun with not working....For a guy
who played the left-wing lock the past eight years, I can say it
was a lot easier for me to wait for my guy to come up toward
me and to lock onto him and ride him into the boards. This
is harder.

–Brendan Shanahan (1969–), New York Rangers left winger

I have had referees say, "You don't want to get a reputation
like Darcy Tucker or Theo Fleury."

–Mike Comrie (1980–), New York Islanders center,
on his temptation to dive

Freddie, what are you doing? If this one lasts much longer,
we're going to miss last call at the bars. Get that guy off the
ice so we can get a cold one before everything is closed.

–John Ashley (1930–2008), NHL referee, to Philadelphia Flyers
head coach Fred Shero after he put his number one goon, Dave
"the Hammer" Schultz, on the ice in the final minute of a game

Everybody's diving now. You used to dive and go back to the
bench, and guys would bitch at you and say: "Come on.
Don't embarrass us." Now you get a high-five.

–Brian Burke (1955–), Anaheim Ducks general manager

It was a nose dive, a swan dive. He flipped backward while he
was doing it.

–Mike Keenan (1949–), Florida Panthers head coach,
on Buffalo Sabres center Daniel Brière

My old man used to tell me, "If you ain't dead, don't lay there."
Maybe a lot of guys didn't have fathers telling them that.

–Kevin Lowe (1959–), Edmonton Oilers general manager,
on players diving

He's going down like free beer at a frat party.

–Pierre McGuire (1961–), Canadian sportscaster, on New York
Islanders right winger Mariusz Czerkawski's frequent diving

THE STRANGE

It is bad enough that there is a disproportional number of mullets being sported in the NHL, but that is just the tip of the iceberg!

I remember what Ron Greschner said when he retired, "The thing I'm going to miss most is showering with 23 guys." And that's what it's all about, camaraderie.

> –Mike Richter (1966–), New York Rangers goaltender

We believe in camaraderie, but that's taking it too far.

> –Rick Bowness (1955–), New York Islanders head coach, on when his player Ziggy Palfy kissed teammate Travis Green on the lips after a goal

I was a multimillionaire from playing hockey. Then I got divorced, and now I am a millionaire.

> –Bobby Hull (1939–), Chicago Blackhawks Hall of Fame left winger

Maybe when I was 11 years old. I took down a couple of figure skating medals back in the day.

> –Colby Armstrong (1982–), Atlanta Thrashers right winger, in answer to the question, "When was the last time you won a medal in something other than hockey?"

Some days, the sun even shines on a dog's butt.

> –Wade Redden (1977–), Ottawa Senators defenseman, on an Ottawa come-from-behind 6–2 win over Toronto

We have to get families back in the game, get back where Saturday night everything stops. A case of beer comes out and a bottle of rye. And anyone who comes to the house, they better want to watch hockey.

> —Bobby Hull (1939–), Chicago Blackhawks Hall of Fame
> left winger

He had better get married soon, because he's getting uglier every day!

> —Mark Recchi (1968–), Atlanta Thrashers right winger, on former
> Philadelphia Flyers teammate Stewart Malgunas

I was 13 or 14 and I met [Donald Trump] at a bar mitzvah of a good friend of ours, who's friends with him. He had his girlfriend at the time, that Melania, with him. He said, "Hey guys, if you work hard and be successful, you'll get one of these." I'll never forget that. And now he's married to her.

> —Jason Spezza (1983–), Ottawa Senators center,
> on the most famous person he's ever met

I was just in the wrong spot at the wrong time. It happens to me all the time.

> —Tuomo Ruutu (1983–), Carolina Hurricanes left winger, on being
> mistakenly arrested as a suspect in an armed robbery case while out
> for a post-practice jog in a black sweatsuit and cap

Ice hockey players can walk on water.

> —Author unknown

Is that a beard, or is Niedermayer eating a muskrat?

> —Harry Neale (1937–), Canadian sportscaster, commenting on
> Rob Niedermayer's facial hair

I've smelled enough sweat. After 61 years, I'm going to give it up. I don't want to stay here till I'm 100. That's too long.

> —Wally Crossman, on his retirement day in 2002, when he was 91 years old. Crossman joined the Red Wings as a locker room assistant in 1940.

Maybe I'm hanging around with Dennis Rodman too much.

> —Dmitri Yushkevich (1971–), Toronto Maple Leafs defenseman, with his bleached blond hair, pondering the idea of dying it blue for the playoffs

Will hit Claude Lemieux from behind for food.

> —Toronto Police, reporting that several witnesses had seen a man carrying a sign with these words on it in the downtown area

I remember one night he called me into his room, and told me that he could feel his thighs growing.

> —Zdenek Chára, father of Zdeno, on his son's incredible height. Zdeno finally stopped growing at 6'9".

Every time I see you naked, I feel sorry for your wife.

> —Jaromir Jágr (1972–), Pittsburgh Penguins right winger, to teammate Matthew Barnaby

What kind of hair did Mel Gibson have in *Braveheart*? It's warrior hair, and hockey players are warriors.

> —Barry Melrose (1956–), coach of the Los Angeles Kings, on the popularity of the mullet in the NHL

If Jaromir Jágr can wear a mullet for eight years, why can't I wear a Mohawk?

> —Bryan McCabe (1975–), Toronto Maple Leafs defenseman, on criticisms over his new hairdo

SOUNDING OFF

*Don Cherry may be renowned for his controversial verbiage,
but he is not alone in a sport where no one holds back from
expressing his opinion—on whatever they feel like!*

Why is a puck called a *puck*? Because *dirty little bastard* was
taken.

> –Martin Brodeur (1972–), New Jersey Devils goaltender

I know of [Parti Québecois leader] Pauline Marois, and I think
she's got bigger things on her plate than talking about Saku
Koivu. And if she doesn't, there's serious problems with the
government in Québec.

> –Alex Tanguay (1979–), Calgary Flames left winger, on the
> mini-controversy about Koivu's failure to speak French
> when introducing his fellow Canadiens at Montréal's
> October 13, 2007, home opener

Listen, I'm trying to stay away from criticizing as far as the
calls, but [expletive] that. I just don't get it. And it makes the
coaching job that much harder, how you coach your players
in playing when you get that [expletive] out there.

> –John Tortorella (1958–), Tampa Bay Lightning head coach, on the
> refereeing in the Atlanta Thrashers' 4–3 overtime win against
> Tampa Bay, November 19, 2007

He's like a freaking zombie in the morning. He doesn't want
to talk much in the mornings.

> –Johan Hedberg (1973–), Atlanta Thrashers goaltender, on
> the breakfast-table demeanor of rookie Swedish teammate
> and current housemate, defenseman Tobias Enstrom

Koivu does it every night. All the refs here should know that he's going to come and touch the goalie at least once a night, or make it look like he got pushed in. It's pretty obvious, and it's every year, every season, every game. I don't see how the refs cannot know players. They ref enough.

–Ryan Miller (1980 –), Buffalo Sabres goaltender, on Montréal captain Saku Koivu's alleged propensity for goaltender interference

Girls, where are you? I can't find you.

–Alexander Ovechkin (1985–), Washington Capitals left winger, on his inability to locate pretty girls while zooming around downtown Washington, D.C., on a Segway with teammates Nicklas Backstrom, Matt Bradley and Mike Green

As opposed to living the rich life and consuming as much as possible, people have to take a step back. Instead of buying the biggest diamond or having 18 cars, do other things. Buying the biggest thing is outdated and there is no excuse for it.

–Andrew Ference (1979–), Boston Bruins defenseman, on his pro-environmental, anti-consumption philosophy

If it's sexy, let's be honest, sex sells. I wouldn't have a problem with that. If they're going to say that every player cheats on his wife, that's just not the case and I'd have an issue with it.

–Shawn Horcoff (1978–), Edmonton Oilers center, on his concerns about a racy, hockey-themed soap opera called *MVP* that premiered on CBC in January 2008. He shouldn't have worried, it was cancelled a few months later.

I'm going through the neutral zone, and I've got a guy tugging me through the whole way. If I don't go down, I'm not going to get a call.

–Paul Kariya (1974–), St. Louis Blues left winger

Guys like him ruin it for everybody else. It's just embarrassing. Or maybe he's not embarrassed because he probably believes he's not doing it—that's how liars are.

> —Chris Chelios (1962–), Detroit Red Wings defenseman,
> on Kariya's remarks

He should be worried about playing the game, not innovating it. He thinks he's Brett Hull or something. You should remind him that he didn't go to college. He's a junior [hockey] guy. So he's not that bright.

> —Garth Snow (1969–), New York Islanders goalie, after hearing
> Philadelphia Flyers center Jeremy Roenick's complaints about
> the officiating in a Flyers-Islanders game

It's not my fault [Snow] didn't have any other options coming out of high school. If going to college gets you a career backup goaltender job, and my route gets you a thousand points and a thousand games, and compare the two contracts, it doesn't take a rocket scientist to figure out whose decision was better.

> —Jeremy Roenick, (1970–), Philadelphia Flyers center, responding

I was surprised by how easy it came out. It was one of those tear-away tongues. Kevin [Lowe, the Edmonton Oilers general manager] said I should have tucked it into the breast pocket of my jacket. Like an ascot.

> —Craig MacTavish (1958–), Edmonton Oilers head coach, after
> ripping the tongue from the head of Calgary Flames mascot
> Harvey the Hound

[Harvey] was in a place he shouldn't have been.

> —Peter Hanlon, Calgary Flames spokesman, who has presumably
> since advised the hound to avoid players benches

I was not very moody. I just do my job and answer [reporters'] questions. I think they never took the chance to get to know me. They say I didn't show up some nights, but how can you say every athlete plays the same all the time? It's not up to me. For the month of January, I didn't play [as many minutes of] hockey at all, until I spoke out, not to the coaches but to the papers. Afterward, they said I was moody. I said, "What can you do on the bench?" Should I be happy on the bench? Sometimes you have to explain things.

–Sergei Fedorov (1969–), Washington Capitals center, at the conclusion of his final season as a Red Wing

I used the N-word instead of calling him Trevor. I used it just not thinking....I told Trev this is an old wound with me. I grew up with it. I am sorry as anybody that it stuck with me.

–John Vanbiesbrouck (1963–), Sault Ste. Marie Greyhounds head coach and general manager, announcing his resignation. Team captain Trevor Daley left the team after hearing of Vanbiesbrouck's comments from other players.

People ask, "Why don't more minorities play hockey?" Well, what are you going to play for? Are you going to play just to get substandard treatment or be treated foolishly or unfairly?

–Kevin Weekes (1975–), Carolina Hurricanes goaltender, a former teammate of Vanbiesbrouck's on the Florida Panthers

Yeah, I saw it. I thought that was great. I didn't know that he was that funny. He has some good material. I have a charity banquet, and with his excellent material, I might ask him to speak.

– Brendan Shanahan (1969–), Detroit Red Wings left winger, responding to a tirade by Vancouver general manager Brian Burke, who claimed the officiating in the Red Wings–Canucks series in the 2002 playoffs favored Detroit

Oh my God, with his wingspan and size, it's like he's 13 feet long.

> —Jeremy Roenick, (1970–), San Jose Sharks center, commenting on the 6'9" frame of defenseman Zdeno Chára

I think he respected my worth as a hockey manager, but he could never admit that my ability for identifying hockey talent and molding a team were far ahead of his.

> —Frank Selke (1893–1985), Montréal Canadiens general manager, on leaving Conn Smythe and the Toronto Maple Leafs

Frank Selke always said for public consumption that he and I parted company because of a trade he made without my permission, while I was overseas. This is not true but probably sounds better, which is why Selke would say it.

> —Conn Smythe (1895–1980), Toronto Maple Leafs owner and hockey builder, responding to Selke's comments

Tell that cocky Junior B goaltender that he won't be facing New York Rangers peashooters when the Leafs open up on him. After we get through with Vachon, he may be back in Junior B.

> —George "Punch" Imlach (1918–87), Toronto Maple Leafs coach and general manager, directing his anger at Montréal Canadiens goaltender Rogatien Vachon

I wouldn't urinate in his ear if his brain was on fire.

> —Bobby Hull, (1939–), Chicago Blackhawks left winger, on a longtime Montréal rival

MIX AND MATCH

And then there are quotes that defy categorization!

I tried to talk my daughter out of going with a hockey player, but he's a good kid. He asked me if he could marry Carrie before he asked her. I said, "You want to what?" I thought he was just going to ask for more ice time.

> –Phil Esposito (1939–), Boston Bruins great, on his daughter
> Carrie getting engaged to Tampa Bay Lightning left winger
> Alexander Selivanov

I know that he often gives only 60 percent of his capacity, but it's hard to punish him because at 60 percent he's better than our other defensemen at 100 percent.

> –Réjean Houle (1949 –), Montréal Canadiens general manager,
> on Canadiens defenseman Vladimir Malakhov

It was always the number one question whenever we talked to people. They'd ask, "When are you going to do a sequel?" I was sure that someday, it would come to fruition.

> –Steve Carlson (1955–), former New England Whalers center and
> one of the "Hanson brothers" in the 1977 film *Slap Shot*, discuss-
> ing the release of the 2002 film *Slap Shot 2: Breaking The Ice*

Come to where?

> –Dave Hanson (1954–), former New England Whalers defenseman
> and Carlson's on-screen brother, responding

Fruition.

> –Carlson, answering

Bill Barilko disappeared that summer
He was on a fishing trip
The last goal he ever scored
Won the Leafs the Cup
They didn't win another
Until 1962
The year he was discovered
I stole this from a hockey card
I keep tucked up under
My fifty mission cap
I worked it in
To look like that

> –Lyrics to "Fifty Mission Cap," a Tragically Hip song about
> the death of Toronto Maple Leafs defenseman Bill Barilko in
> a plane crash. Barilko disappeared on a fishing trip in 1951.
> The wreckage of his plane was only discovered, as the song
> indicates, in 1962.

I'd rather tame a tiger than paint stripes on a kitty cat.

> –Dean Lombardi (1958–), San Jose Sharks general manager, on
> obtaining frequently suspended player Bryan Marchment from
> the Tampa Bay Lightning in March 1998

NOTES ON SOURCES

Allen, Kevin and Bob Duff. *Without Fear: Hockey's 50 Greatest Goaltenders*. Chicago: Triumph Books, 2002.

Dryden, Ken. *The Game*. Toronto: Wiley Press, 2005.

Goyens, Chrys and Allan Turowetz. *Lions in Winter*. Scarborough: Prentice-Hall, 1986.

Hunter, Douglas. *A Breed Apart*. Toronto: Viking Press, 1995.

Joyce, Gare. *Sidney Crosby: Taking the Game by Storm*. Markham: Fitzhenry & Whiteside, 2007.

Leonetti, Mike. *Canadiens Legends: Montreal's Hockey Heroes*. Vancouver: Raincoast Books, 2003.

Podnieks, Andrew, et al. *Kings of the Ice: A History of World Hockey*. Richmond Hill: NDE Publishing, 2002.

Web Sources

http://www.quotegarden.com/hockey.html

http://www.quoteland.com/topic.asp?CATEGORY_ID=213

http://www.brainyquote.com/quotes/keywords/hockey.html

http://proicehockey.about.com/lr/hockey_quotes/141972/1/

J. Alexander Poulton

J. Alexander Poulton is a writer and photographer and has been a genuine enthusiast of Canada's national pastime ever since seeing his first hockey game. His favorite memory was meeting the legendary gentleman hockey player Jean Béliveau, who in 1988 towered over the young awe-struck author.

He earned his B.A in English Literature from McGill University and his graduate diploma in Journalism from Concordia University. He has 14 other sports books to his credit, including books on hockey, soccer and baseball.